DATA AND INFORMATION SCIENCE

DATA AND INFORMATION SCIENCE

Dr. S. Mangairkarasi
Associate Professor,
Dept of CSE, Sathyabama Institute
of Science and Technology

Dr. N. Senthamilarasi
Associate Professor,
Dept of CSE, Sathyabama Institute
of Science and Technology

Dr. V. Subapriya
Associate Professor,
Dept of CSE, Sathyabama Institute
of Science and Technology

KHANNA BOOK PUBLISHING CO. (P) Ltd.
4C/4344, Ansari Road, Darya Ganj,
New Delhi, India

Sathyabama Institute of Science and Technology
Jeppiaar Nagar, Rajiv Gandhi Salai,
Chennai, Tamilnadu, India

Dear Readers,

To prevent the piracy, this book is secured with HIGH SECURITY HOLOGRAM on the front title cover. In case you don't find the hologram on the front cover title, please write us to at contact@khannabooks.com or whatsapp us at +91-99109 09320 and avail special gift voucher for yourself.

Specimen of Hologram on front Cover title:

Moreover, there is a SPECIAL DISCOUNT COUPON for you with EVERY HOLOGRAM.

How to avail this SPECIAL DISCOUNT:

Step 1: Scratch the hologram
Step 2: Under the scratch area, your "coupon code" is available
Step 3: Logon to www.khannabooks.com
Step 4: Use your "coupon code" in the shopping cart and get your copy at a special discount
Step 5: Enjoy your reading!

Thanks,
Khanna Publishing House

ISBN: 978-93-55389-72-5

DATA AND INFORMATION SCIENCE

by **Dr. S. Mangairkarasi**
Dr. N. Senthamilarasi
Dr. V. Subapriya

First Edition: 2026

To view complete list of books, please scan the QR Code:

Published by:
Khanna Book Publishing Co. (P) Ltd.
CIN: U22110DL1998PTC095547

Visit us at: www.khannabooks.com
Write us at: contact@khannabooks.com

Printed in Bharat.

Preface

In a rapidly evolving digital age, data is becoming an essential ingredient for modern innovation growth and decision making. Nowadays, enterprises, governments and individuals all need to be able to use data to gather analyze and draw results. This is not only competitive advantage. An indepth understanding of the key concepts, techniques and tools that support the transformative area is the goal of this book on data and information science. Computer science, statistics, machine learning and domain specific expertise are all combined in the multidisciplinary area of the data science. Information science on the other hand, focuses on the collection, organization, dissemination and utilization of information. When taken together, these two studies enable us detect patterns, predict results nd ultimately make better decisions.

The basic concepts of date management, data visualization, algorithms and machine learning will be discussed in this book, along with more complex subjects like artificial intelligence big data analytics and data ethics. We seek to close the gap between theory and practice by looking at real world case studies, providing both technical and strategic insights.

The process of converting raw data into information that can be put to use is include several steps, such as data collection, cleaning, analyzis and interpretation. With a focus on understanding both the opportunities and limitations of these technologies, we will give readers the tools and techniques necessary to successfully navigate each step. The intended audience for this book includes professionals, hobbyists and students. We believe this material will be a useful resource for learning and a practical advice for anybody new to the field of data and information science or looking to expand their knowledge. Giving you the skills to critically interact with data in meaningful ways and utilize it to spur creativity and problem solving in your profession is the utilimate goal. The material of these pages will help you not only comprehend the present but also actively influence the direction of data and information science as we approach a data driven revolution.

Contents

UNIT 1

Data Acquisition

1.1 INTRODUCTION

What is Data?

Data

- a piece of raw information, facts, or numbers collected to be examined or analyzed
- to make decisions.
- should be in a formalized manner suitable for communication, interpretation, and processing.

Information

- Result of analyzing data

Types of Data

- **Structured:** Data that is organized and formatted in a specific way that forms a well-defined schema or shape to form a proper structure.
- **Unstructured:** These data are unorganized and context-specific or varying. Eg., e-mail
- **Natural language:** It is a special type of unstructured data; it's challenging to process because it requires knowledge of specific data science techniques and linguistics
- **Machine-generated:** data automatically created by a computer, process, application, or other machine without human intervention.
- **Graph-based:** data that focuses on the relationship or adjacency of objects
- **Audio, video, and images:** captured and recognized through sound, pictures and videos
- **Streaming:** Data flows into the system when an event occurs instead of being loaded into a data store in a batch.

Data File Formats

- Tabular (e.g., .csv, .tsv, .xlsx)
- Non-tabular (e.g., .txt, .rtf, .xml)
- Image (e.g., .png, .jpg, .tif)

- Agnostic (e.g., .dat)
- some file formats are **proprietary** and can only be opened by software developed by a particular company
- Other file formats store metadata, such as SPSS and STATA files which contain information on data labels.

Data versus Information

***Table 1.1:** Difference between Data and Information*

S. No.	Data	Information
1.	Data are the variables that help to develop ideas/conclusions.	Information is meaningful data.
2.	Data are text and numberical values.	Information is refined form of actual data.
3.	Data doesn't rely on information.	While information relies on Data.
4.	Bits and Bytes are the measuring unit of data.	Information is measured in meaningful units like time, quantity, etc.
5.	Data is collection of facts, which itself have no meaning.	Information puts those facts info context.

1.2 DATA ACQUISITION

Data Acquisition

- The process of gathering various data from different relevant sources is referred to as Data Acquisition
- It translates into the collection of data and ingesting it into a system for further use.

Importance of Data Acquisition

- It is easier for businesses to analyze and formulate corresponding strategies around it.
- Having data in one place makes it easier to detect any discrepancy and solve it faster.
- It also decreases human error and improves data security.
- In the longer run, it proves to be cost-efficient.
- It helps in building a Recommendation System

Data acquisition comprises two steps – **Data Harvest** and **Data Ingestion**

1. Data Harvest

It is the process by which a source generates data and it considers what data is acquired.

2. Data Ingestion

- Focuses on bringing the produced data into a given system.
- Data ingestion consists of three stages – discover, connect, and synchronize.

Data Acquisition Methods

Data can be obtained from many different sources, such as websites, apps, IoT protocols or even physical notes, and new data sources pop up literally every day.

Methods of Acquiring Data

- Collecting new data.
- Converting and/or transforming legacy data.
- Sharing or exchanging data.
- Purchasing data.

Challenges and Characteristics to be Considered for Data Acquisition

Every data acquisition method comes with additional challenges and characteristics to be considered. For example, when it comes to transforming legacy data, first assess the legacy quality. And for purchasing data, all the licensing issues need to be analyzed.

For specific domains, heavily regulated industries like banking, or a government-controlled entity, additional restrictions may also apply– for instance, data standard thresholds or business rule limitations.

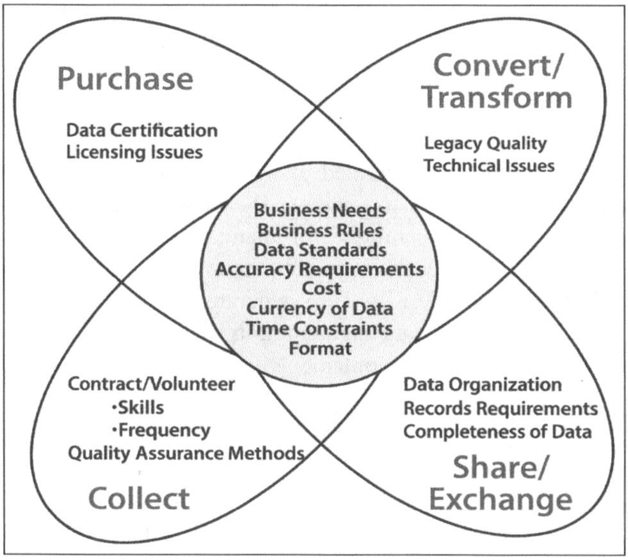

Figure 1.1: *Data Acquisition Process*

Data Acquisition in Machine Learning

"Data acquisition is the process of sampling signals that measure real-world physical conditions and converting the resulting samples into digital numeric values that a computer can manipulate."

- **Collection and Integration of the data:** The data is extracted from various sources and multiple data need to be combined based upon the requirement.
- **Formatting:** Prepare or organize the datasets as per the analysis requirements.
- **Labeling:** After gathering data, it is required to label or name the data

Data Acquisition Process

The process of data acquisition involves searching for the datasets that can be used to train the Machine Learning models.

The main segments are:

1. Data Discovery
2. Data Augmentation
3. Data Generation

1. Data Discovery

The first approach for acquiring data is Data discovery. It is a key step when indexing, sharing, and searching for new datasets available on the web and incorporating data lakes. It can be broken into two steps: Searching and Sharing. Firstly, the data must be labeled or indexed and published for sharing using many available collaborative systems for this purpose.

2. Data Augmentation

The next approach for data acquisition is Data augmentation. Augment means to make something greater by adding to it, so here in the context of data acquisition, we are essentially enriching the existing data by adding more external data. In Deep and Machine learning, using pre-trained models and embeddings is common to increase the features to train on.

3. Data Generation

As the name suggests, the data is generated. If we do not have enough and any external data is not available, the option is to generate the datasets manually or automatically. Crowdsourcing is the standard technique for manual construction of the data where people are assigned tasks to collect the required data to form the generated dataset. There are automatic techniques available as well to generate synthetic datasets. Also, the data generation method can be seen as data augmentation when there is data available however it has missing values that need to be imputed.

1.3 SOURCES OF ACQUIRING DATA

Data collection is the process of acquiring, collecting, extracting, and storing a voluminous amount of data which may be in structured or unstructured form like text, video, audio, XML files, records, or other image files used in later stages of data analysis. In the process of big data analysis, "Data collection" is the initial step before starting to analyze the patterns or useful information in data. The data which is to be analyzed must be collected from different valid sources.

There are four methods of acquiring data:

1. collecting new data;
2. converting/transforming legacy data;
3. sharing/exchanging data;
4. purchasing data.

This includes the automated collection (e.g., of sensor-derived data), the manual recording of empirical observations, and obtaining existing data from other sources

Data Acquisition Techniques and Tools

The major tools and techniques for data acquisition are:

1. Data Warehouses and ETL
2. Data Lakes and ELT
3. Cloud Data Warehouse providers

1. Data Warehouses and ETL

The first option to acquire data is via a data warehouse. Data warehousing is the process of constructing and using a data warehouse to offer meaningful business insights. A data warehouse is a centralized repository, which is constructed by combining data from various heterogeneous sources. It is primarily created and used for data reporting and analysis rather than transaction processing. The focus of the data warehouse is on the business processes.

A data warehouse is typically constructed to store structured records having tabular formats. Employees' data, sales records, payrolls, student records, and CRM all come under this bucket. In a data warehouse, usually, we transform the data before loading, and hence, it falls under the approach of ETL (Extract, Transform, and Load). It is defined as the extraction of data, the transformation of data, and the loading of the data.

The data acquisition is performed by two kinds of ETL (Extract, Transform, and Load), these are:

(a) **Code-based ETL:** These ETL applications are developed using programming languages such as SQL, and PL/SQL (which is a combination of SQL and procedural features of programming languages). Examples: BASE SAS, SAS ACCESS.

(b) **Graphical User Interface (GUI)-based ETL:** This type of ETL application are developed using the graphical user interface, and point and click techniques. Examples are data stage, data manager, AB Initio, Informatica, ODI (Oracle Data Integration), data services, and SSIS (SQL Server Integration Services).

2. Data Lakes and ELT

A data lake is a storage repository having the capacity to store large amounts of data, including structured, semi-structured, and unstructured data. It can store images, videos, audio, sound records, and PDF files. It helps for faster ingestion of new data. Unlike data warehouses, data lakes store everything, are more flexible, and follow the Extract, Load, and Transform (ELT) approach. The data is first loaded and not transformed until required to transform. Therefore, the data is processed later as per the requirements. Data lakes provide an "unrefined view of data" to data scientists. Open-source tools such as Hadoop and Map Reduce are available under data lakes.

3. Cloud Data Warehouse Providers

A cloud data warehouse is another service that collects, organizes, and stores data. Unlike traditional data warehouses, cloud data warehouses are quicker and cheaper to set up as no physical hardware needs to be procured. Additionally, these architectures use massively parallel processing (MPP), i.e., employ a large number of computer processors (up to 200 or more processors) to perform a set of coordinated computations in parallel simultaneously and, therefore, perform complex analytical queries much faster.

Some of the prominent cloud data warehouse services are:

- Amazon Redshift
- Snowflake
- Google Big Query
- IBM Db2 Warehouse
- Microsoft Azure Synapse
- Oracle Autonomous Data Warehouse
- SAP Data Warehouse Cloud
- Yellowbrick Data
- Teradata Integrated Data Warehouse

Primary Data

Primary data refers to the data originated by the researcher for the first time

- Conducting research and experiments, surveys and simulations are common methods for acquiring primary data.
- Web scraping is also a special case of primary data collection by extracting or copying data directly from a website.

Examples: Survey, Interview, Questionnaire, Observations etc.,

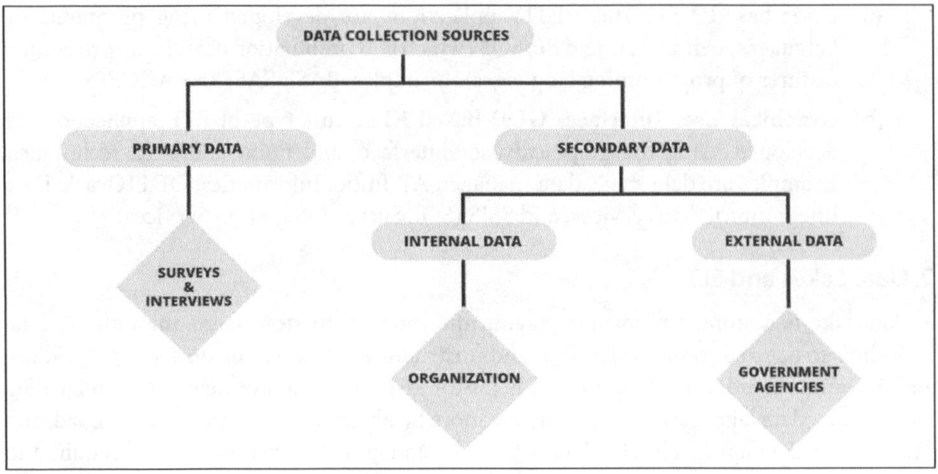

Figure 1.2: Sources of Data

Secondary Data

- Secondary data is the already existing data collected by the investigator agencies and organizations earlier.

It can be obtained from many different websites and also from Application Programming Interface. Some of the most popular repositories include:

- GitHub
- Kaggle
- KDnuggets

- UCI Machine Learning Repository
- US Government's Open Data
- Five Thirty-Eight
- Amazon Web Services
- BuzzFeed

1.4 INTERNAL SYSTEMS AND EXTERNAL SYSTEMS

Internal Systems

- Internal data is generated and used within a company or organization.
- This data is usually produced by the company's operations, such as sales, customer service, or production.
- Internal data occurs in various formats, such as spreadsheets, databases, or customer relationship management (CRM) systems.

Examples of internal data:

- *Users data* – logs, messages, mails etc.,
- *Internal documents* – invoices, contracts, notes etc.,
- *IoT devices* – cameras, sensors etc.,
- *Logs* – website/platform logs

External Systems

- Data collected from external sources, including customers, partners, competitors, and industry reports.
- This data can be purchased from third-party providers or gathered from publicly available sources including market research reports, social media data, government data etc.,

Examples of External Data

- *Web* – e-commerce, real estate etc.,
- *Geo* – maps, location, GPS etc.,
- *Files* – invoices, documents, sheets etc.,
- *Third parties* – weather, credit card, telecom etc.,

1.5 WEB APIS

Application Programming Interface (API) - a set of defined rules that enable different applications to communicate with each other.

Basic Elements of an API

- **Access:** allowed to use the data or services
- **Request:** is the actual data or service being asked for
- **Response:** the data or service as a result of a request

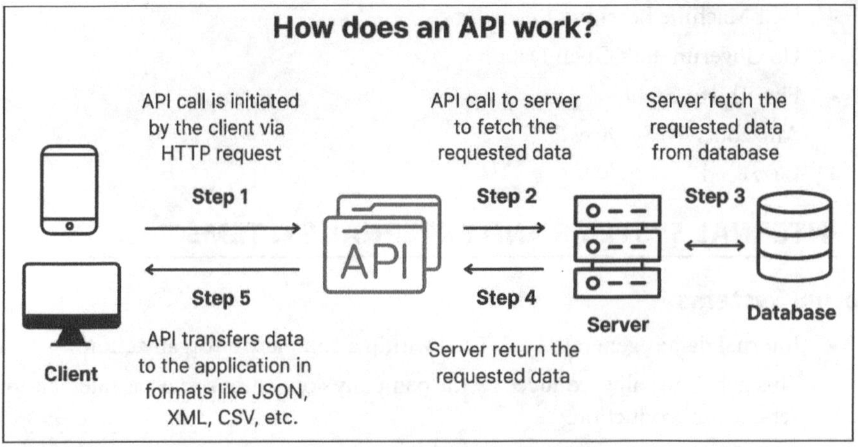

Figure 1.3: *Process of API*

Web APIs

- A Web API is an interface to either a web server or a web browser.
- These APIs are used extensively for the development of web applications.
- These APIs work at either the server end or the client end.
- Companies like Google, Amazon, eBay all provide web-based API.
- Some popular examples of web-based API are Twitter REST API, Facebook Graph API, Amazon S3 REST API, etc.

REST API

REST stands for **RE**presentational **S**tate **T**ransfer. It is a web architecture with a set of constraints applied to web service applications. REST APIs provide data in the form of resources that can be related to objects.

Some of the popular APIs in ML and Data Science

1. Google Map API

Google Map API is one of the commonly used API. Its applications vary from integration in a cab service application to the popular Pokemon Go. It supports to retrieve all the information like location coordinates, distances between locations, routes etc.

2. Amazon Machine Learning API

This API is used for developers to build applications like fraud detection, targeted marketing, and demand forecasting. These APIs create machine learning models by finding the trends in provided data with great accuracy.

3. Facebook API

Facebook API provides an interface to a large amount of data generated every day. The innumerable post, comments and shares in various groups & pages produce massive data. And this massive public data provides a large number of opportunities for analyzing the crowd. It is also incredibly convenient to use Facebook Graph API with both R and Python to extract data.

5. Twitter API

Just like Facebook Graph API, Twitter data can be accessed using the Twitter API as well. We can access all the data like tweets made by any user, tweets containing a particular term or even a combination of terms, tweets done on the topic in a particular date range, etc. Twitter data is a great resource for performing the tasks like opinion mining, and sentiment analysis.

6. IBM Watson API

IBM Watson offers a set of APIs for performing a host of complex tasks such as Tone analyzer, document conversion, personality insights, visual recognition, text-to-speech, speech-to-text, etc by using just a few lines of code. This set of APIs differs from the other APIs discussed so far, as they provide a service for manipulating and deriving insights from the data.

6. US Census Bureau API

This API allows to make custom queries to the data and embed them into mobile or web applications. Census usually contains data on the population and economy of a nation. This data can be used to make major demographic and economic statistics more accessible to users.

7. Quandl API

Quandl helps to invoke the time series information of a large number of stocks for the specified date range. The setting up of Quandl API is very easy and provides a great resource for projects like Stock price prediction, stock profiling, etc.

1.6 DATA PRE-PROCESSING

Data preprocessing is an important process of data mining. In this process, raw data is converted into an understandable format and made ready for further analysis. The motive is to improve data quality and make it up to mark for specific tasks.

Purpose of Data Preprocessing

After properly gathering the data, it needs to be explored, or assessed, to spot key trends and inconsistencies. The main goals of Data preprocessing are:

- **Get data overview:** understand the data formats and overall structure in which the data is stored. Also, find the properties of data like mean, median, standard quantiles, and standard deviation. These details can help identify irregularities in the data.
- **Identify missing data:** missing data is common in most real-world datasets. It can disrupt true data patterns, and even lead to more data loss when entire rows and columns are removed because of a few missing cells in the dataset.
- **Identify outliers or anomalous data:** some data points fall far out of the predominant data patterns. These points are outliers and might need to be discarded to get predictions with higher accuracies unless the primary purpose of the algorithm is to detect anomalies.

- **Remove Inconsistencies:** just like missing values, real-world data also has multiple inconsistencies like incorrect spellings, incorrectly populated columns, and rows (eg.: salary populated in gender column), duplicated data, and much more. Sometimes, these inconsistencies can be treated through automation, but most often they need a manual check-up.

Tasks in Data Preprocessing

- **Data Cleaning:** Data cleaning helps us remove inaccurate, incomplete, and incorrect data from the dataset. Some techniques used in data cleaning are –
- **Handling missing values:** This type of scenario occurs when some data is missing. Standard values can be used to fill up the missing values in a manual way but only for a small dataset. Attribute's mean and median values can be used to replace the missing values in normal and non-normal distribution of data respectively. Tuples can be ignored if the dataset is quite large and many values are missing within a tuple.
- The most appropriate value can be used while using regression or decision tree algorithms

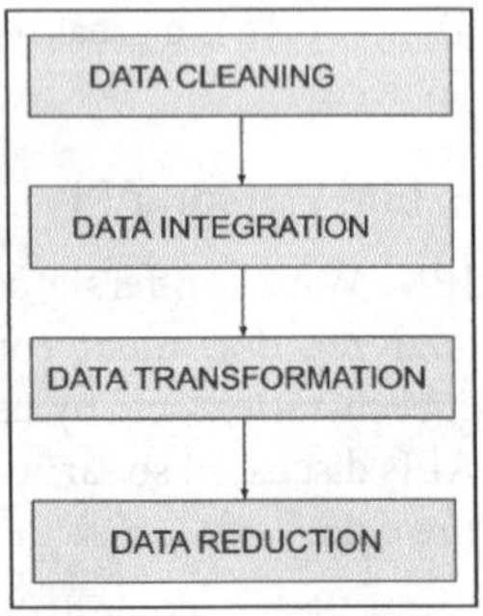

Figure 1.4: Steps of Data Preprocessing

- **Noisy Data:** Noisy data are data that cannot be interpreted by machines and contain unnecessary faulty data. Some ways to handle them are –
  - **Binning:** This method handles noisy data to make it smooth. Data gets divided equally and stored in the form of bins and then methods are applied to smoothing or completing the tasks. The methods are Smoothing by a bin mean method (bin values are replaced by mean values), Smoothing by bin median (median values replace bin values) and Smoothing by bin boundary(minimum/maximum bin values are taken and replaced by closest boundary values).
  - **Regression:** Regression functions are used to smoothen the data. Regression can be linear (consists of one independent variable) or multiple (consists of multiple independent variables).
  - **Clustering:** It is used for grouping similar data in clusters and is used for finding outliers.

Data Integration

The process of combining data from multiple sources (databases, spreadsheets, text files) into a single dataset. A single and consistent view of data is created in this process. Major problems during data integration are Schema integration (Integrates a set of data collected from various sources), Entity identification (identifying entities from different databases), and detecting and resolving data values concept.

Data Transformation

The change made in the format or the structure of the data is called data transformation. This step can be simple or complex based on the requirements. There are some methods for data transformation.

- **Smoothing:** With the help of algorithms, we can remove noise from the dataset and help in knowing the important features of the dataset. By smoothing we can find even a simple change that helps in prediction.
- **Aggregation:** In this method, the data is stored and presented in the form of a summary. The data set which is from multiple sources is integrated into with data analysis description. This is an important step since the accuracy of the data depends on the quantity and quality of the data. When the quality and the quantity of the data are good the results are more relevant.
- **Discretization:** The continuous data here is split into intervals. Discretization reduces the data size. For example, rather than specifying the class time, we can set an interval like (3 pm-5 pm, 6 pm-8 pm).
- **Normalization:** It is the method of scaling the data so that it can be represented in a smaller range. Example ranging from -1.0 to 1.0.
- **Attribute Selection:** To help the mining process, new attributes are derived from the given attributes.
- **Concept Hierarchy Generation:** In this, the attributes are changed from a lower level to higher level in hierarchy.

Data Reduction

It helps in increasing storage efficiency and reducing data storage to make the analysis easier by producing almost the same results. Analysis becomes harder while working with huge amounts of data, so the reduction is used to get rid of that.

Steps of data reduction are:

1. Data Compression

The compressed form of data is called data compression. Data is compressed to make efficient analysis. This compression can be lossless or lossy. Lossless compression is when there is no loss of data while compression. lossy compression is when unnecessary information is removed during compression.

2. Numerosity Reduction

There is a reduction in the volume of data i.e. only store model of data instead of whole data, which provides a smaller representation of data without any loss of data.

3. Dimensionality Reduction

This process is necessary for real-world applications as the data size is big. In this process, the reduction of random variables or attributes is done so that the dimensionality of the data set can be reduced.

Combining and merging the attributes of the data without losing its original characteristics. This also helps in the reduction of storage space and computation time is reduced. In this, reduction of attributes or random variables are done to make the data set dimension low.

Data preprocessing in Machine Learning: A Practical Approach

Data preprocessing is a process of preparing the raw data and making it suitable for a machine learning model. It is the first and crucial step in creating a machine learning model.

A real-world data generally contains noises, and missing values, and may be in an unusable format that cannot be directly used for machine learning models. Data preprocessing is a required task for cleaning the data and making it suitable for a machine learning model which also increases the accuracy and efficiency of a machine learning model.

It involves below steps:

- Getting the dataset
- Importing libraries
- Importing datasets
- Finding Missing Data
- Encoding Categorical Data
- Splitting dataset into training and test set
- Feature scaling

1. Get the Dataset

To create a machine learning model, the first thing we required is a dataset as a machine learning model completely works on data. The collected data for a particular problem in a proper format is known as the **dataset**. The dataset may be of different formats for different purposes, such as, if we want to create a machine learning model for business purposes, then the dataset will be different from the dataset required for a liver patient. So each dataset is different from another dataset. To use the dataset in our code, we usually put it into a CSV **file**. However, sometimes, we may also need to use an HTML or xlsx file.

What is a CSV File?

CSV stands for "**Comma-Separated Values**" files; it is a file format that allows us to save tabular data, such as spreadsheets. It is useful for huge datasets and can be used in programs.

Here we will use a demo dataset for data preprocessing, and for practice, it can be downloaded from kaggle open source. We can also create our dataset by gathering data using various API with Python and put that data into a .csv file.

2. Importing Libraries

In order to perform data preprocessing using Python, we need to import some predefined Python libraries. These libraries are used to perform some specific jobs. There are three specific libraries that we will use for data preprocessing, which are:

- **Numpy:** The Numpy Python library is used for including any type of mathematical operation in the code. It is the fundamental package for scientific calculation in Python. It also supports to add large, multidimensional arrays and matrices. So, in Python, we can import it as:

1. Import Numpy as Nm

Here we have used **nm**, which is a short name for Numpy, and it will be used in the whole program.

- **Matplotlib:** The second library is **matplotlib**, which is a Python 2D plotting library, and with this library, we need to import a sub-library **pyplot**. This library is used to plot any type of charts in Python for the code. It will be imported as below:

2. Import Matplotlib.pyplot as Mpt

Here we have used mpt as a short name for this library.

- **Pandas:** The last library is the Pandas library, which is one of the most famous Python libraries and used for importing and managing the datasets. It is an open-source data manipulation and analysis library. It will be imported as below:

Here, we have used pd as a short name for this library.

Consider the below image:

```
# importing libraries
import numpy as nm
import matplotlib.pyplot as mtp
import pandas as pd
```

3. Importing the Datasets

Now we need to import the datasets that we have collected for our machine learning project. But before importing a dataset, we need to set the current directory as a working directory.

To set a working directory in Spyder IDE, we need to follow the below steps:

- Save your Python file in the directory that contains the dataset.
- Go to File Explorer option in Spyder IDE, and select the required directory.
- Click on F5 button or run option to execute the file.

Here, in the below image, we can see the Python file along with the required dataset. Now, the folder is set as a working directory.

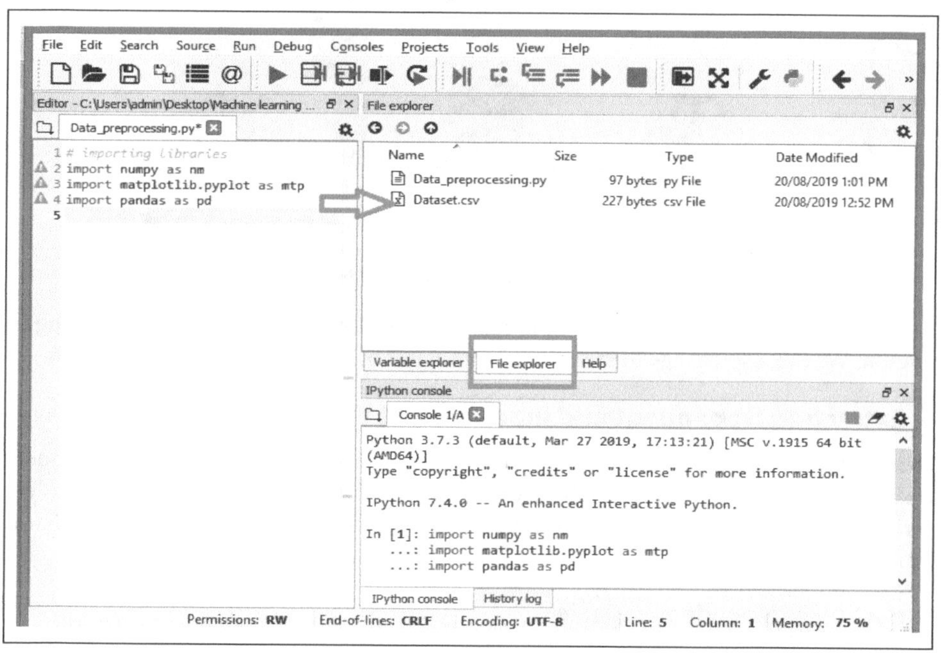

Figure 1.5: *Loading Dataset*

read_csv() function

Now to import the dataset, we will use the read_csv() function of the pandas library, which is used to read a csv file and perform various operations on it. Using this function, we can read a csv file locally as well as through a URL.

We can use read_csv function as below:

1. data_set= pd.read_csv('Dataset.csv')

Here, data_set is a name of the variable to store our dataset, and inside the function, we have passed the name of our dataset. Once we execute the above line of code, it will successfully import the dataset in our code. We can also check the imported dataset by clicking on the section variable explorer, and then double click on data_set. Consider the below image:

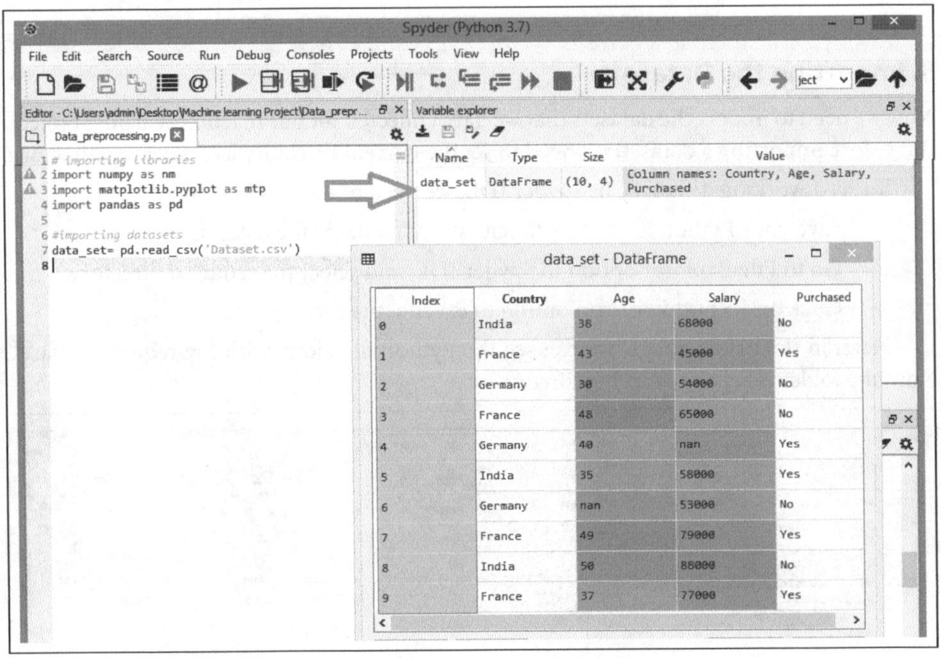

Figure 1.6: Changing the Format of the Data Set

As in the above image, indexing is started from 0, which is the default indexing in Python. We can also change the format of our dataset by clicking on the format option.

4. Extracting Dependent and Independent Variables

In machine learning, it is important to distinguish the matrix of features (independent variables) and dependent variables from dataset. In our dataset, there are three independent variables that are **Country, Age**, and **Salary**, and one is a dependent variable which is **Purchased.**

Extracting Independent Variable

To extract an independent variable, we will use **iloc[ ]** method of Pandas library. It is used to extract the required rows and columns from the dataset.

```
1. x= data_set.iloc[:,:-1].values
```

In the above code, the first colon(:) is used to take all the rows, and the second colon(:) is for all the columns. Here we have used :-1, because we don't want to take the last column as it contains the dependent variable. So by doing this, we will get the matrix of features.

By executing the above code, we will get output as:

```
1. [['India' 38.0 68000.0]
2. ['France' 43.0 45000.0]
3. ['Germany' 30.0 54000.0]
4. ['France' 48.0 65000.0]
5. [Germany' 40.0 nan]
6. ['India' 35.0 58000.0
7. ['Germany' nan 53000.0]
8. ['France' 49.0 79000.0]
9. ['India' 50.0 88000.0]
10. ['France' 37.0 77000.0]]
```

As we can see in the above output, there are only three variables.

Extracting Dependent Variable

To extract dependent variables, again, we will use the Pandas. iloc[] method.

```
1. y= data_set.iloc[:,3].values
```

Here we have taken all the rows with the last column only. It will give the array of dependent variables. By executing the above code, we will get the output as:

array(['No', 'Yes', 'No', 'No', 'Yes', 'Yes', 'No', 'Yes', 'No', 'Yes'], dtype=object)

5. Handling Missing Data

The next step of data preprocessing is to handle missing data in the datasets. If our dataset contains some missing data, then it may create a huge problem for our machine learning model. Hence it is necessary to handle missing values present in the dataset.

Ways to handle missing data: There are mainly two ways to handle missing data, which are:

- **By deleting the particular row:** The first way is used to commonly deal with null values. In this way, we just delete the specific row or column which consists of null values.

  But this way is not so efficient and removing data may lead to loss of information which will not give the accurate output.

- **By calculating the mean:** In this way, we will calculate the mean of that column or row which contains any missing value and will put it on the place of missing value. This strategy is useful for the features that have numeric data such as age, salary, year, etc. Here, we will use this approach.

To handle missing values, we will use Scikit-learn library in our code, which contains various libraries for building machine learning models. Here we will use Imputer class of sklearn.preprocessing library.

Below is the code for it:

```
#handling missing data (Replacing missing data with the mean value)
from sklearn.preprocessing import Imputer
imputer= Imputer(missing_values ='NaN', strategy='mean', axis = 0)
#Fitting imputer object to the independent variables x.
imputerimputer= imputer.fit(x[:, 1:3])
#Replacing missing data with the calculated mean value
x[:, 1:3]= imputer.transform(x[:, 1:3])
```

Output

```
array([['India', 38.0, 68000.0],
['France', 43.0, 45000.0],
['Germany', 30.0, 54000.0],
['France', 48.0, 65000.0],
['Germany', 40.0, 65222.22222222222],
['India', 35.0, 58000.0],
['Germany', 41.111111111111114, 53000.0],
['France', 49.0, 79000.0],
['India', 50.0, 88000.0],
['France', 37.0, 77000.0]], dtype=object
```

As we can see in the above output, the missing values have been replaced with the means of rest column values.

6. Encoding Categorical Data

Categorical data is data which has some categories such as, in our dataset; there are two categorical variable, **Country**, and **Purchased**. Since machine learning model completely works on mathematics and numbers, but if our dataset would have a categorical variable, then it may create trouble while building the model. So it is necessary to encode these categorical variables into numbers.

For Country Variable

Firstly, we will convert the country variables into categorical data. So to do this, we will use **LabelEncoder()** class from the **preprocessing** library.

```
#Catgorical data
#for Country Variable
from sklearn.preprocessing import LabelEncoder
 label_encoder_x= LabelEncoder()
x[:, 0]= label_encoder_x.fit_transform(x[:, 0])
```

Output

```
Out[15]:
array([[2, 38.0, 68000.0],
[0, 43.0, 45000.0],
[1, 30.0, 54000.0],
[0, 48.0, 65000.0],
[1, 40.0, 65222.22222222222],
```

```
[2, 35.0, 58000.0],
[1, 41.111111111111114, 53000.0],
[0, 49.0, 79000.0],
[2, 50.0, 88000.0],
[0, 37.0, 77000.0]], dtype=object)
```

Explanation

In above code, we have imported **LabelEncoder** class of **sklearn library**. This class has successfully encoded the variables into digits. But in our case, there are three country variables, and as we can see in the above output, these variables are encoded into 0, 1, and 2. By these values, the machine learning model may assume that there is some correlation between these variables which will produce the wrong output. So to remove this issue, we will use **dummy encoding**.

Dummy Variables

Dummy variables are those variables which have values 0 or 1. The 1 value gives the presence of that variable in a particular column, and rest variables become 0. With dummy encoding, we will have several columns equal to the number of categories. In our dataset, we have 3 categories so it will produce three columns having 0 and 1 values. For Dummy Encoding, we will use the **OneHotEncoder** class of **preprocessing** library.

```
#for Country Variable
from sklearn.preprocessing import LabelEncoder, OneHot
Encoder
 label_encoder_x= LabelEncoder()
x[:, 0]= label_encoder_x.fit_transform(x[:, 0])
 #Encoding for dummy variables
onehot_encoder=OneHotEncoder(categorical_features= [0])
 x= onehot_encoder.fit_transform(x).toarray()
```

Output

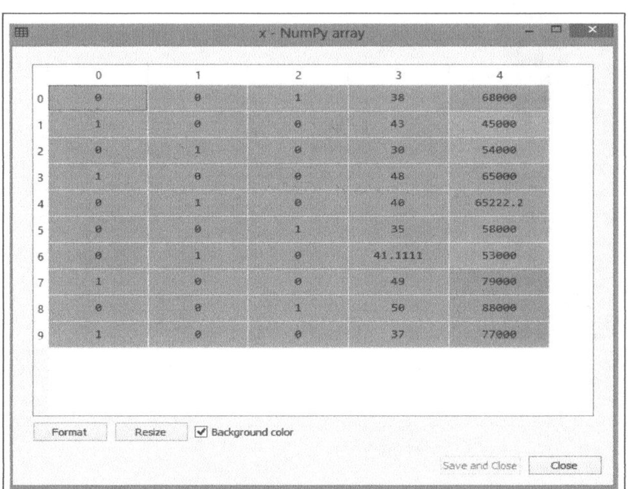

	0	1	2	3	4
0	0	0	1	38	68000
1	1	0	0	43	45000
2	0	1	0	30	54000
3	1	0	0	48	65000
4	0	1	0	40	65222.2
5	0	0	1	35	58000
6	0	1	0	41.1111	53000
7	1	0	0	49	79000
8	0	0	1	50	88000
9	1	0	0	37	77000

Figure 1.7: *Dummy Variables*

```
array([[0.00000000e+00,       0.00000000e+00,       1.00000000e+00,
3.80000000e+01, 6.80000000e+04],
[1.00000000e+00,  0.00000000e+00,  0.00000000e+00,  4.30000000e+01,
4.50000000e+04],
[0.00000000e+00,  1.00000000e+00,  0.00000000e+00,  3.00000000e+01,
5.40000000e+04],
[1.00000000e+00,  0.00000000e+00,  0.00000000e+00,  4.80000000e+01,
6.50000000e+04],
[0.00000000e+00,  1.00000000e+00,  0.00000000e+00,  4.00000000e+01,
6.52222222e+04],
[0.00000000e+00,  0.00000000e+00,  1.00000000e+00, 3.50000000e+01,
5.80000000e+04],
[0.00000000e+00,  1.00000000e+00,  0.00000000e+00,  4.11111111e+01,
5.30000000e+04],
```

As we can see in the above output, all the variables are encoded into numbers 0 and 1 and divided into three columns. It can be seen more clearly in the variable's explorer section, by clicking on x option as

For Purchased Variable

```
labelencoder_y= LabelEncoder()
y= labelencoder_y.fit_transform(y)
```

For the second categorical variable, we will only use label encoder object of the **LableEncoder** class. Here we are not using the **One Hot Encoder** class because the purchased variable has only two categories yes or no, and which are automatically encoded into 0 and 1.

Output

Out[17]: array([0, 1, 0, 0, 1, 1, 0, 1, 0, 1])

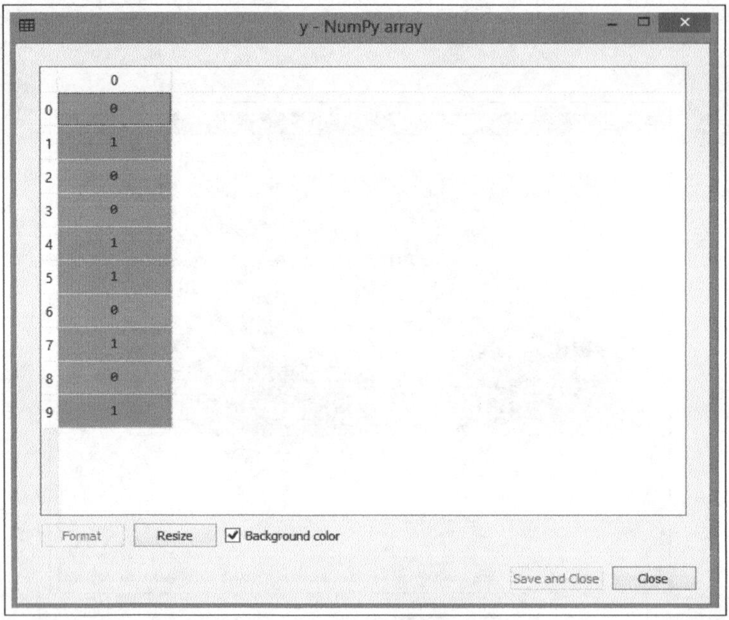

Figure 1.8: *Encoded Format*

7. Splitting the Dataset Into The Training Set and Test Set

In machine learning data preprocessing, we divide our dataset into a training set and test set. This is one of the crucial steps of data preprocessing as by doing this, we can enhance the performance of our machine learning model.

Suppose, if we have given training to our machine learning model by a dataset and we test it by a completely different dataset. Then, it will create difficulties for our model to understand the correlations between the models.

If we train our model very well and its training accuracy is also very high, but we provide a new dataset to it, then it will decrease the performance. So we always try to make a machine learning model which performs well with the training set and also with the test dataset. Here, we can define these datasets as:

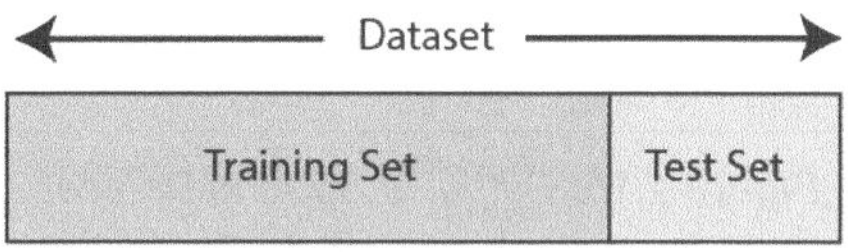

Figure 1.9: *Structure of Data Set*

- **Training Set:** A subset of dataset to train the machine learning model, and we already know the output.
- **Test set:** A subset of dataset to test the machine learning model, and by using the
- test set, model predicts the output.

For splitting the dataset, we will use the below lines of code:

```
from sklearn.model_selection import train_test_split
x_train, x_test, y_train, y_test= train_test_split(x, y, test_size= 0.2, random_state=0)
```

Explanation

- In the above code, the first line is used for splitting arrays of the dataset into random train and test subsets.
- In the second line, we have used four variables for our output that are
- **x_train:** features for the training data
- **x_test:** features for testing data
- **y_train:** Dependent variables for training data
- **y_test:** Independent variable for testing data
- In train_test_split() function, we have passed four parameters in which first two are for arrays of data, and test_size is for specifying the size of the test set.

  The test_size maybe .5, .3, or .2, which tells the dividing ratio of training and testing sets.
- The last parameter random_state is used to set a seed for a random generator so that you always get the same result, and the most used value for this is 42.

Output

By executing the above code, we will get 4 different variables, which can be seen under the variable explorer section.

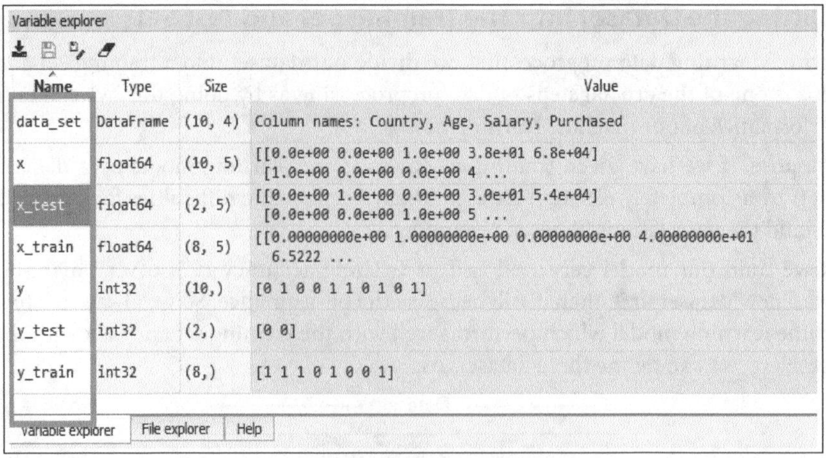

Figure 1.10: *Output of Splitting Dataset*

As we can see in the above image, the x and y variables are divided into 4 different variables with corresponding values.

8. Feature Scaling

Feature scaling is the final step of data preprocessing in machine learning. It is a technique to standardize the independent variables of the dataset in a specific range. In feature scaling, we put our variables in the same range and in the same scale so that no any variable dominate the other variable.

- **Consider the below dataset:** As we can see, the age and salary column values are not on the same scale. A machine learning model is based on **Euclidean distance**, and if we do not scale the variable, then it will cause some issue in our machine learning model.

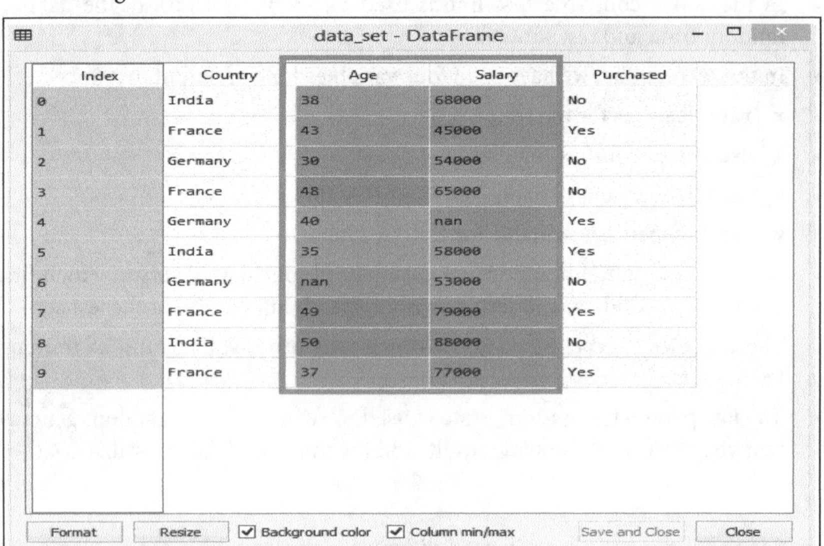

Figure 1.11: *Feature Scaling*

Euclidean distance is given as:

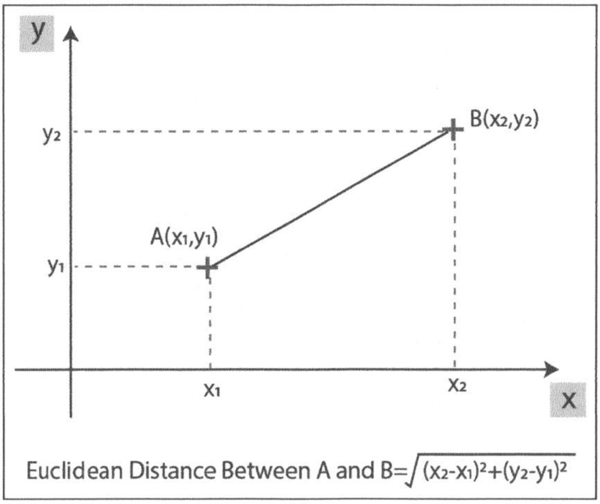

Figure 1.12: *Euclidian Distance*

If we compute any two values from age and salary, then salary values will dominate the age values, and it will produce an incorrect result. So to remove this issue, we need to perform feature scaling for machine learning.

There are two ways to perform feature scaling in machine learning:

Standardization

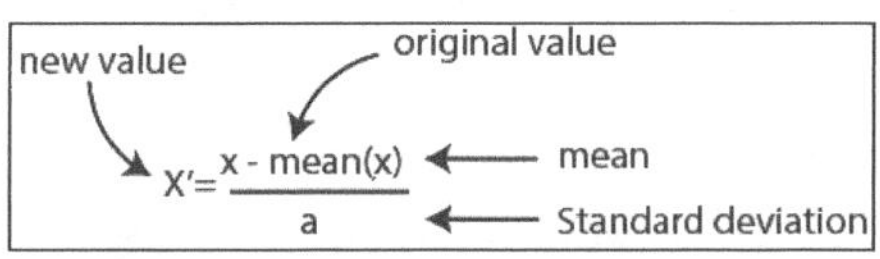

Figure 1.13: *Euclidian Distance*

Normalization

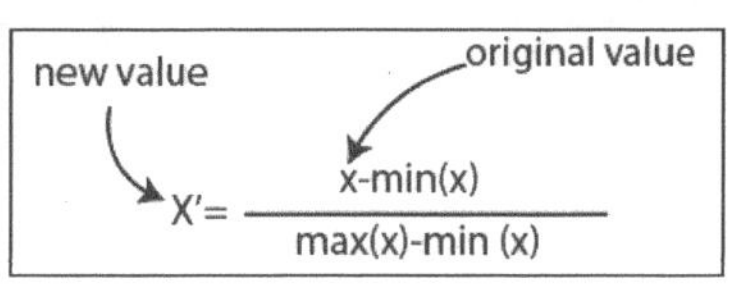

Figure 1.14: *Euclidian Distance*

Here, we will use the standardization method for our dataset.

For feature scaling, we will import StandardScaler class of sklearn.preprocessing library as:

from sklearn.preprocessing import StandardScaler

Now, we will create the object of **StandardScaler** class for independent variables or features. And then we will fit and transform the training dataset.

```
st_x= StandardScaler()
x_train= st_x.fit_transform(x_train)
For test dataset, we will directly apply transform() function instead of fit_transform() because it is already done in training set.
x_test= st_x.transform(x_test)
```

x_train

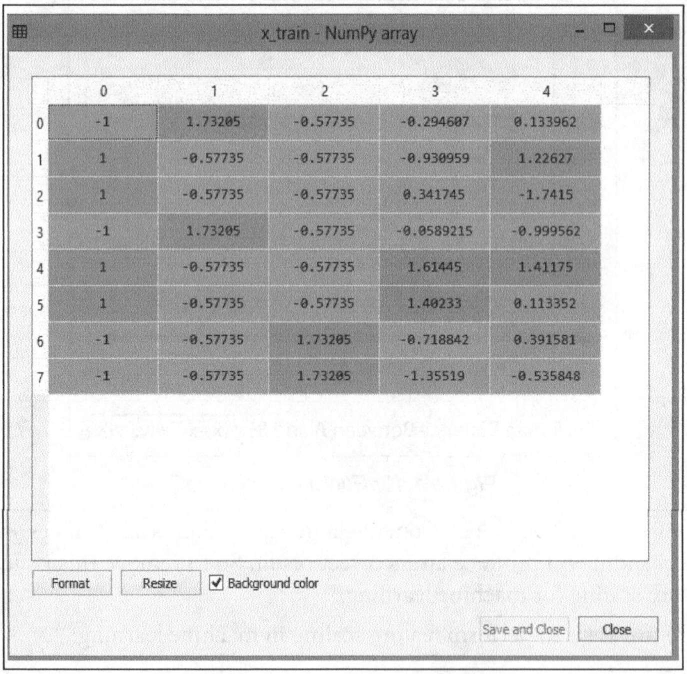

	0	1	2	3	4
0	-1	1.73205	-0.57735	-0.294607	0.133962
1	1	-0.57735	-0.57735	-0.930959	1.22627
2	1	-0.57735	-0.57735	0.341745	-1.7415
3	-1	1.73205	-0.57735	-0.0589215	-0.999562
4	1	-0.57735	-0.57735	1.61445	1.41175
5	1	-0.57735	-0.57735	1.40233	0.113352
6	-1	-0.57735	1.73205	-0.718842	0.391581
7	-1	-0.57735	1.73205	-1.35519	-0.535848

Figure 1.15: *Scaled value for x_train*

x_test

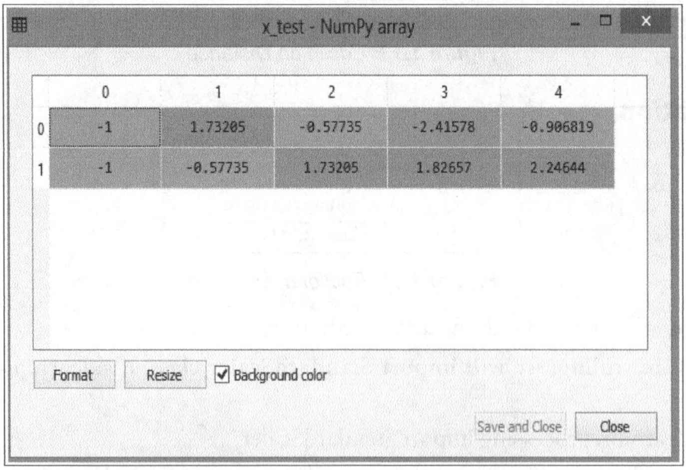

	0	1	2	3	4
0	-1	1.73205	-0.57735	-2.41578	-0.906819
1	-1	-0.57735	1.73205	1.82657	2.24644

Figure 1.16: *Scaled value for x_test*

1.7 EXPLORATORY DATA ANALYSIS

Exploratory Data Analysis is an approach in analyzing data sets to summarize their main characteristics, often using statistical graphics and other data visualization methods. EDA assists Data science professionals in various ways:

1. Getting a better understanding of data
2. Identifying various data patterns
3. Getting a better understanding of the problem statement

Types of Exploratory Data Analysis

There are four primary types of EDA:

- **Univariate non-graphical:** This is simplest form of data analysis, where the data being analyzed consists of just one variable. Since it's a single variable, it doesn't deal with causes or relationships. The main purpose of univariate analysis is to describe the data and find patterns that exist within it.
- **Univariate graphical:** Non-graphical methods don't provide a full picture of the data. Graphical methods are therefore required. Common types of univariate graphics include:
  - Stem-and-leaf plots, which show all data values and the shape of the distribution.
  - Histograms, a bar plot in which each bar represents the frequency (count) or proportion (count/total count) of cases for a range of values.
  - Box plots, which graphically depict the five-number summary of minimum, first quartile, median, third quartile, and maximum.
- **Multivariate nongraphical:** Multivariate data arises from more than one variable. Multivariate non-graphical EDA techniques generally show the relationship between two or more variables of the data through cross-tabulation or statistics.
- **Multivariate graphical:** Multivariate data uses graphics to display relationships between two or more sets of data. The most used graphic is a grouped bar plot or bar chart with each group representing one level of one of the variables and each bar within a group representing the levels of the other variable.

Other common types of multivariate graphics include:

- Scatter plot, which is used to plot data points on a horizontal and a vertical axis to show how much one variable is affected by another.
- Multivariate chart, which is a graphical representation of the relationships between factors and a response.
- Run chart, which is a line graph of data plotted over time.
- Bubble chart, which is a data visualization that displays multiple circles (bubbles) in a two-dimensional plot.
- Heat map, which is a graphical representation of data where values are depicted by color.

1.8 EXPLORATORY DATA ANALYSIS TOOLS

Some of the most common data science tools used to create an EDA include:

- **Python:** An interpreted, object-oriented programming language with dynamic semantics. Its high-level, built-in data structures, combined with dynamic typing and dynamic binding, make it very attractive for rapid application development, as well as for use as a scripting or glue language to connect existing components together. Python and EDA can be used together to identify missing values in a data set, which is important so you can decide how to handle missing values for machine learning.

R

An open-source programming language and free software environment for statistical computing and graphics supported by the R Foundation for Statistical Computing. The R language is widely used among statisticians in data science in developing statistical observations and data analysis.

Line Plot

Line Plot a type of plot which displays information as a series of **data points** called "markers" **connected by straight lines.** In this type of plot, we need the measurement points to be **ordered** (typically by their x-axis values). This type of plot is often used to visualize a trend in data over interval softime-a **time series.** To make a line plot with Matplotlib, we call plt. plot(). The first argument is used for the data on the horizontal axis, and the second is used for the data on the vertical axis.

This function generates your plot, but it doesn't display it. To display the plot, we need to call the plt.show() function. This is nice because we might want to add some additional customizations to our plot before we display it. For example, we might want to add labels to the axis and title for the plot.

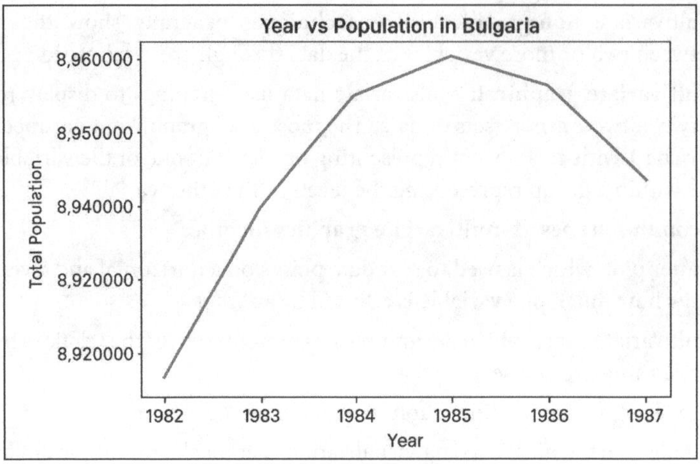

Figure 1.17: Sample Line Plot

Scatter Plot

Scatter Plot this type of plot shows all individual data points. Here, they aren't connected with lines. Each data point has the value of the x-axis value and the value from the y-axis values. This type of plot can be used to display trends or correlations. In data science, it shows how 2 variables compare. To make a scatter plot with Matplotlib, we can use the plt. scatter() function.

Again, the first argument is used for the data on the horizontal axis, and the second - for the vertical axis. Simple Scatter Plot.

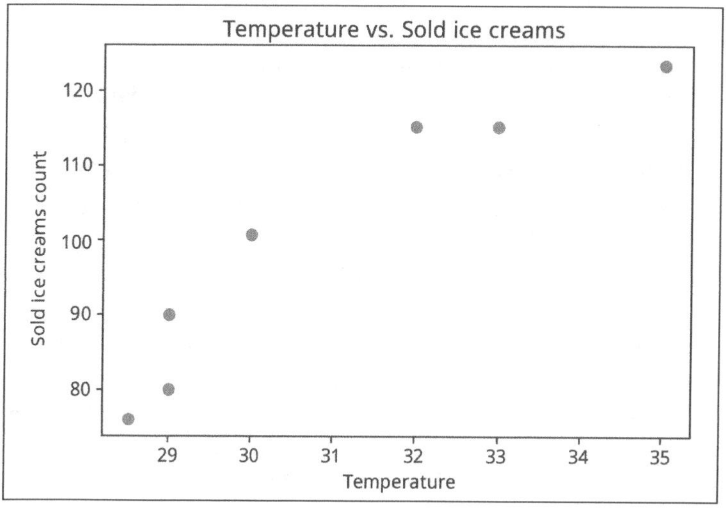

Figure 1.18: *Sample Scatter Plot*

Histogram

Histogram an accurate representation of the distribution of numeric data. To create a histogram, first, we divide the entire range of values into a series of intervals, and second, we count **how many values fall into each interval**. The intervals are also called **bins**. The bins are consecutive and non-overlapping intervals of a variable. They must be adjacent and are often of equal size. To make a histogram with Matplotlib, we can use the plt.hist() function. The first argument is the numeric data, the second argument is the number of bins. The default value for the bins argument is 10.

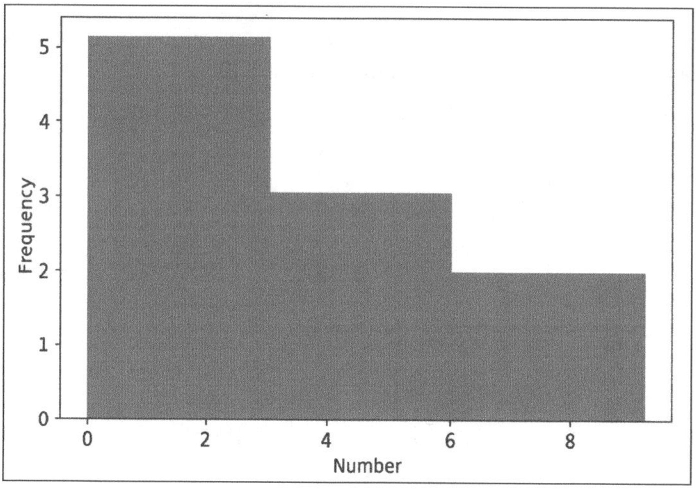

Figure 1.19: *Sample Histogram*

We can see from the histogram above that there are:

- 5 values between 0 and 3
- 3 values between 3 and 6 (including)
- 2 values between 6 (excluding) and 9

Box Plot

Box plot, also called the **box-and-whisker plot**: a way to show the distribution of values based on the five-number summary: **minimum, first quartile, median, third quartile,** and **maximum.**

- **The minimum** and **the maximum** are just the min and max values from our data.
- **The median** is the value that separates the higher half of a data from the lower half.

It's calculated by the following steps: **order your values**, and find the **middle one**. In a case when our count of values is even, we actually have 2 middle numbers, so the median here is calculated by summing these 2 numbers and divide the sum by 2. For example, if we have the numbers 1, 2, 5, 6, 8, 9, your **median** will be (5 + 6) / 2 = 5.5.

- **The first quartile** is the **median** of the **data values to the left** of the median in our ordered values. For example, if we have the numbers 1, 3, 4, 7, 8, 8, 9, the first quartile is the median from the 1, 3, 4 values, so it's 3.
- **The third quartile** is the **median** of the **data values to the right** of the median in our ordered values. For example, if we use these numbers 1, 3, 4, 7, 8, 8, 9 again, the third quartile is the median from the 8, 8, 9 values, so it's 8.
- I also want to mention one more statistic here. That is the **IQR (Interquartile Range)**. The IQR approximates the amount of spread in the middle 50% of the data. The **formula** is **the third quartile - the first quartile.**
- This type of plot can also show **outliers.** An outlier is a data value that lies **outside the overall pattern.** They are visualized as **circles.** When we have outliers, the **minimum** and the **maximum** are visualized as the min and the max values from the values which aren't outliers. There are many ways to identify what is an outlier.
- A commonly used rule says that a value is an outlier if it's **less** than **the first quartile - 1.5** IQR or high than the third quartile + 1.5 * IQR.

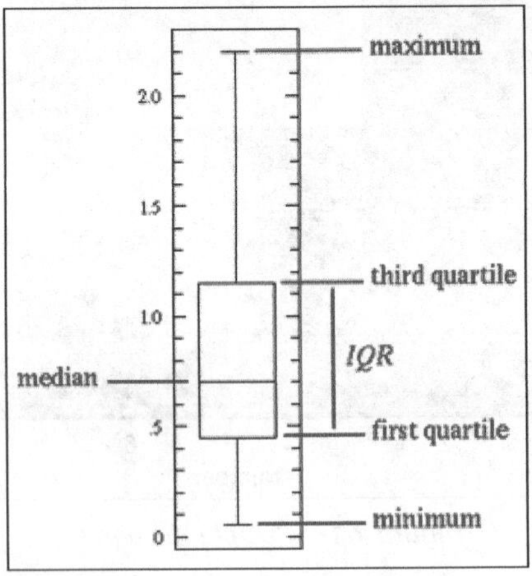

Figure 1.20: *Sample Box Plot*

Now, when we have some knowledge about the box plots, we can see that it's super easy to create this plot with Matplotlib. All we need is the function plt.boxplot(). The first argument is the data points.

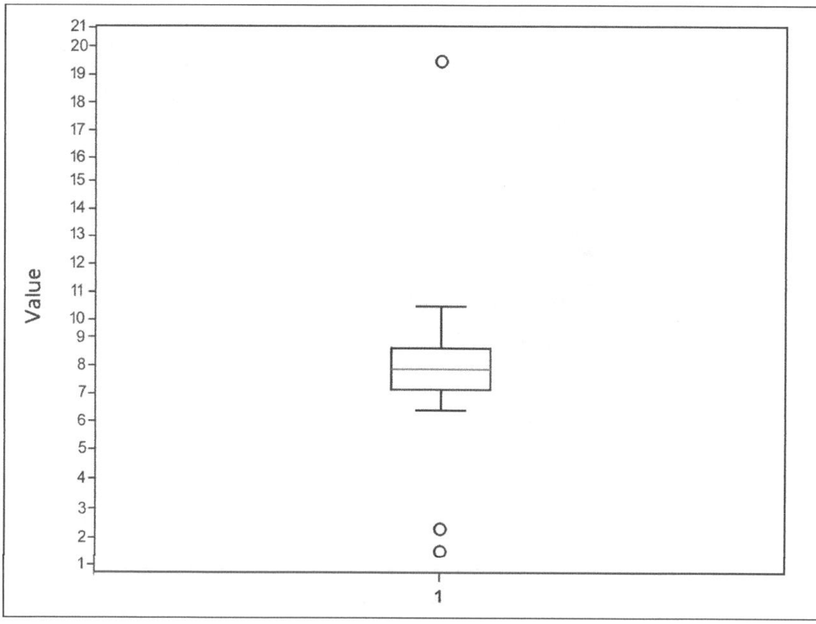

Figure 1.21

In this example the values 1, 2, and 21 are **outliers**, the **maximum** is 10, the **minimum** is 5. And, the **mean** is 7.

Bar Chart

Represents categorical data with rectangular bars. Each bar has a height that corresponds to the value it represents. It's useful when we want to compare a given numeric value on different categories. It can also be used with 2 data series,. To make a bar chart with Maplotlib, we'll need the plt.bar() function.

Simple Bar Chart

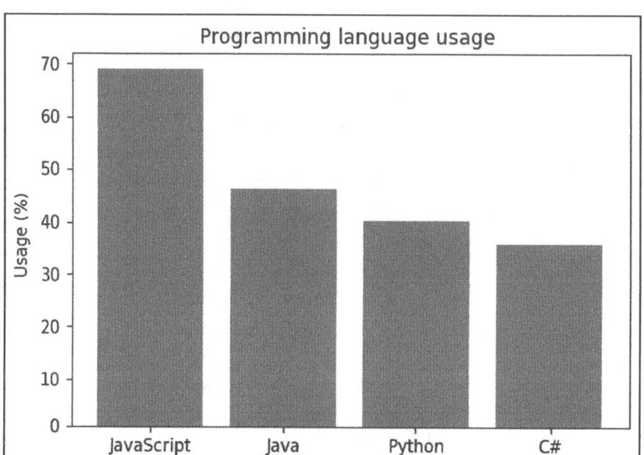

Figure 1.22: *Simple Bar Chart*

Pie Chart

A circular plot, divided into slices to show numerical proportion. They are widely used in the **business world**. However, many experts recommend to **avoid them**. The main reason is that it's difficult to compare the sections of a given pie chart. Also, it's difficult to compare data across multiple pie charts. In many cases, they can be **replaced** by a **bar chart**.

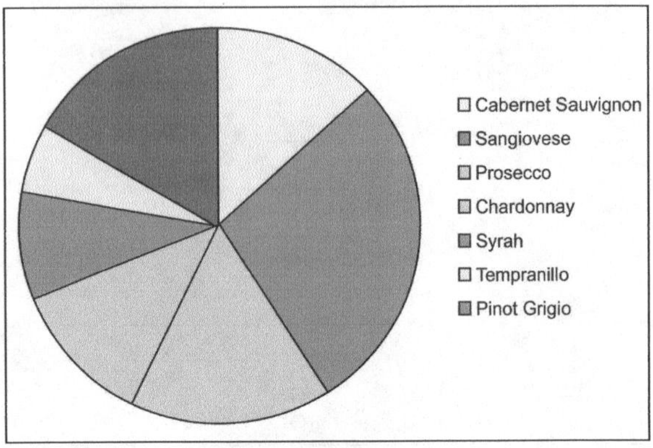

Figure 1.23

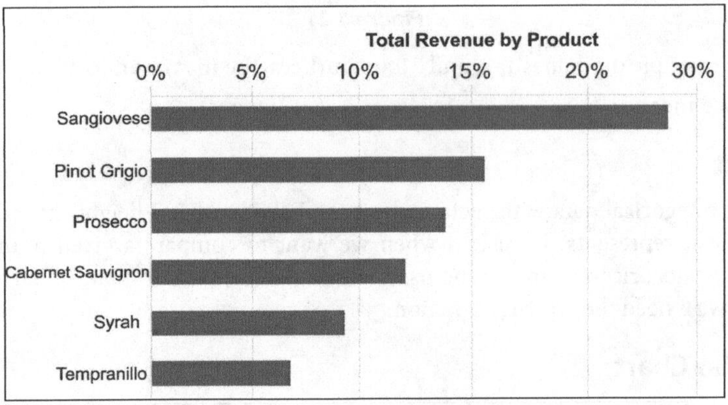

Figure 1.24: *Simple Bar Chart*

To make a pie chart with Matplotlib, we can use the plt.pie() function. The autopct parameter allows us to display the percentage value using the Python string formatting.

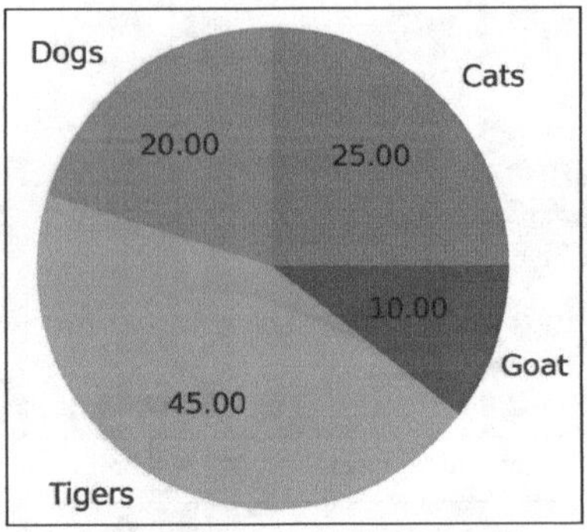

Figure 1.25: *Simple Pie Chart*

Bar and Column Charts

It's one of the simplest graphs to understand how our quantitative field is performing across various categories. It is used for **comparison**.

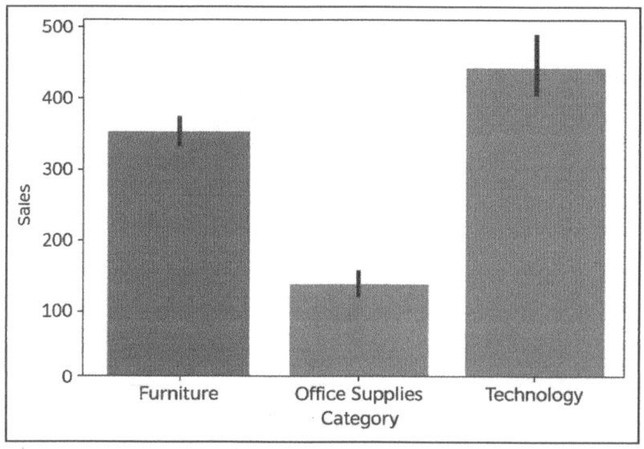

Figure 1.26

From the above column chart, we can see that sales of technology are higher and office supplies are the least.

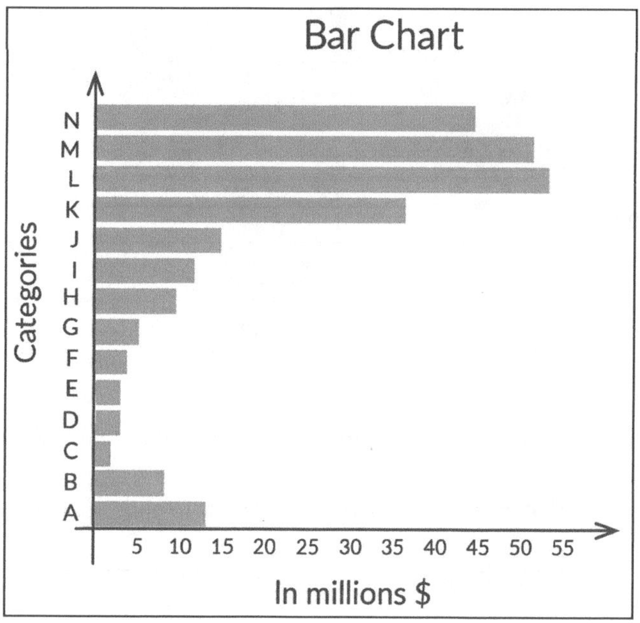

Figure 1.27: *Simple Column and Bar Chart*

Scatter Plot and Bubble Chart

Scatter and bubble plots help us to understand how variables are **spread** across the range considered. It can be used to identify the patterns, the presence of outliers, and the **relationship** between the two variables.

We can see that with the increase in discount, profits are decreasing.

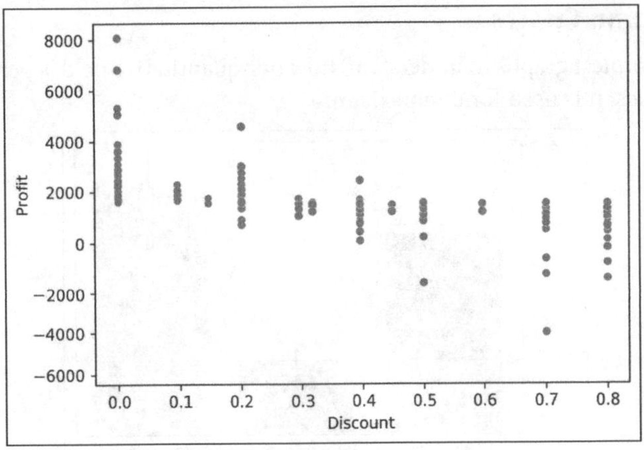

Figure 1.28

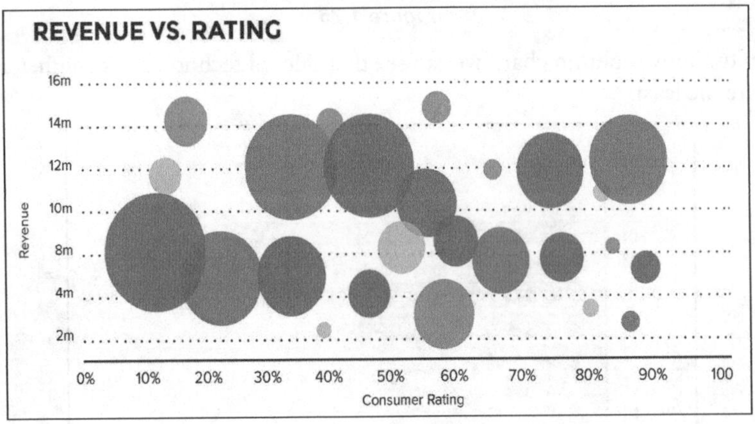

Figure 1.29: *Simple Bubble Chart*

Subplots

Sometimes it's better to plot **different plots** in the same grid to understand and **compare** the data better.

Here you can see that in the single graph we were able to understand sales over a period of time in different regions.

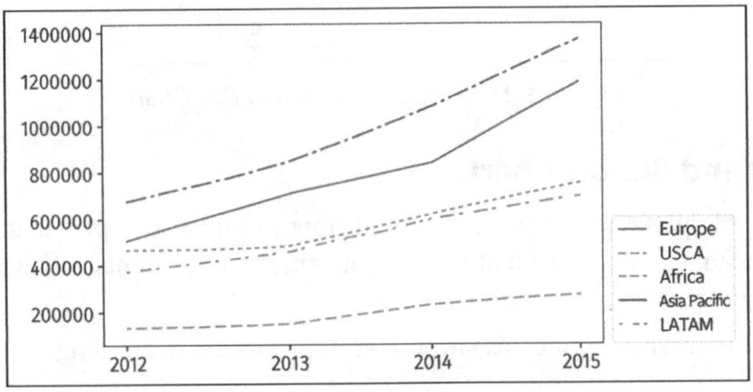

Figure 1.30

Donut, Pie charts and Stacked Column Charts

When we want to find the **composition** of data above-mentioned charts is the best.

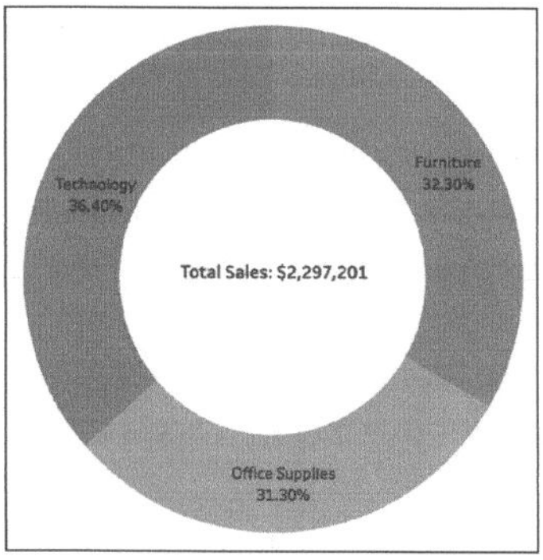

Figure 1.31: *Simple doughnut chart*

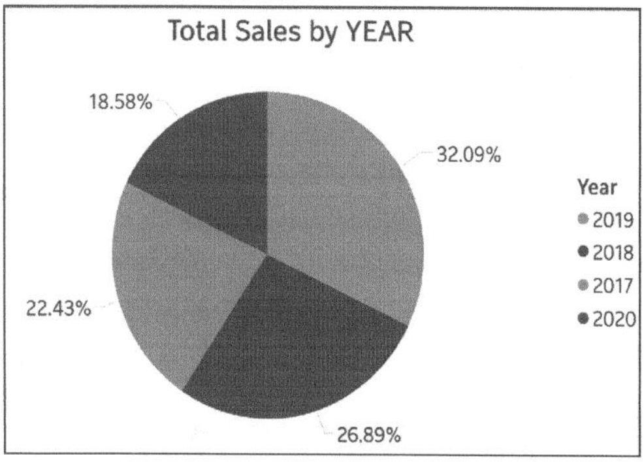

Figure 1.32: *Simple pie chart*

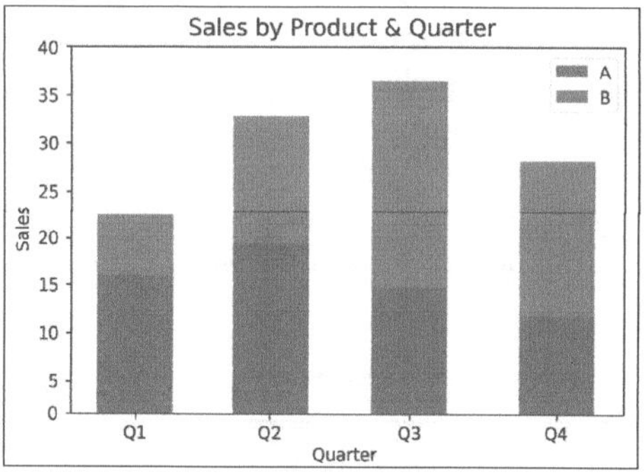

Figure 1.33: *Simple stacked column chart*

Heatmaps

It is the most preferred chart when we want to check if any **correlation** between variables.

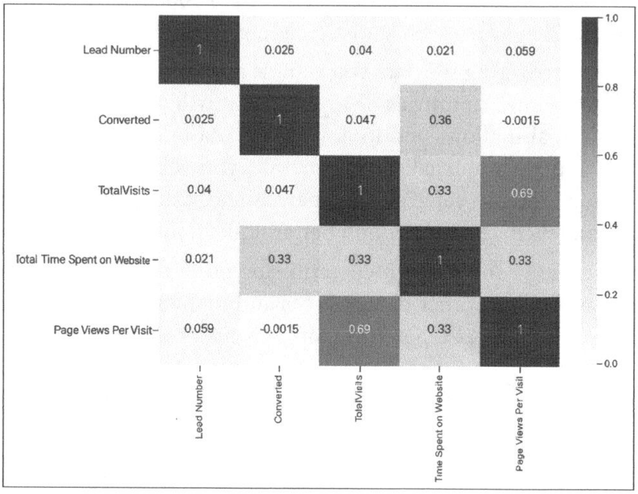

Figure 1.34: *Simple Heatmaps*

Here the positive value shows a positive correlation and the negative value shows a negative correlation. The color indicates the intensity of the correlation, the darker the color higher the positive correlation, and the lighter the color higher the negative correlation.

Open Data

Open Data means the kind of data which is open for anyone and everyone for access, modification, reuse, and sharing.

Open Data derives its base from various "open movements" such as open source, open hardware, open government, open science etc.

Governments, independent organizations, and agencies have come forward to open the floodgates of data to create more and more open data for free and easy access.

Why Is Open Data Important?

Open data is important because the world has grown increasingly data-driven. But if there are restrictions on the access and use of data, the idea of data-driven business and governance will not be materialized. Therefore, open data has its own unique place. It can allow a fuller understanding of the global problems and universal issues. It can give a big boost to businesses. It can be a great impetus for machine learning. It can help fight global problems such as disease or crime or famine. Open data can empower citizens and hence can strengthen democracy. It can streamline the processes and systems that the society and governments have built. It can help transform the way we understand and engage with the world.

1.9 LIST OF 15 AWESOME OPEN DATA SOURCES

World Bank Open Data

As a repository of the world's most comprehensive data regarding what's happening in different countries across the world, World Bank Open Data is a vital source of Open Data. It also provides access to other datasets as well which are mentioned in the data catalog.

World Bank Open Data is massive because it has got 3000 datasets and 14000 indicators encompassing microdata, time series statistics, and geospatial data.

Accessing and discovering the data you want is also quite easy. All you need to do is to specify the indicator names, countries or topics and it will open up the treasure- house of Open Data for you. It also allows you to download data in different formats such as CSV, Excel, and XMLIf you are a journalist or academic, you will be enthralled by the array of tools available to you. You can get access to analysis and visualization tools that can bolster your research. It can felicitate a deeper and better understanding of global problems.

You can get access to the API which can help you create the data visualizations you need, live combinations with other data sources and many more such features. Therefore, it's no surprise that World Bank Open Data tops any list of Open Data sources!

WHO (World Health Organization) — Open data repository

WHO's Open Data repository is how WHO keeps track of health-specific statistics of its 194 Member States. The repository keeps the data systematically organized. It can be accessed as per different needs. For instance, whether it is mortality or burden of diseases, one can access data classified under 100 or more categories such as the Millennium Development Goals (child nutrition, child health, maternal and reproductive health, immunization, HIV/AIDS, tuberculosis, malaria, neglected diseases, water and sanitation), non communicable diseases and risk factors, epidemic-prone diseases, health systems, environmental health, violence and injuries, equity etc. For your specific needs, you can go through the datasets according to themes, category, indicator, and country. The good thing is that it is possible to download whatever data you need in Excel Format. You can also monitor and analyze data by making use of its data portal.

Google Public Data Explorer

Launched in 2010, Google Public Data Explorer can help you explore vast amounts of public-interest datasets. You can visualize and communicate the data for your respective uses. It makes the data from different agencies and sources available.

For instance, you can access data from World Bank, U. S. Bureau of Labor Statistics and U.S. Bureau, OECD, IMF, and others. Different stakeholders access this data for a variety of purposes. Whether you are a student or a journalist, whether you are a policy maker or an academic, you can leverage this tool in order to create visualizations of public data.

You can deploy various ways of representing the data such as line graphs, bar graphs, maps and bubble charts with the help of Data Explorer. The best part is that you would find these visualizations quite dynamic. It means that you will see them change over time. You can change topics, focus on different entries and modify the scale. It is easily shareable too. As soon as you get the chart ready, you can embed it on your website or blog or simply share a link with your friends.

Registry of Open Data on AWS (RODA)

This is a repository containing public datasets. It is data which is available from AWS resources. As far as RODA is concerned, you can discover and share the data which is publicly available. In RODA, you can use keywords and tags for common types of data such as genomic, satellite imagery and transportation in order to search whatever data that you are looking for. All of this is possible on a simple web interface. For every dataset, you will discover detail page, usage examples, license information and tutorials or applications that use this data. By making use of a broad range of compute and data analytics products, you can analyze the open data and build whatever services you want. While the data you access is available through AWS resources, you need to bear in mind that it is not provided by AWS. This data belongs to different agencies, government organizations, researchers, businesses and individuals.

European Union Open Data Portal

You can access whatever open data EU institutions, agencies and other organizations publish on a single platform namely European Union Open Data Portal. The EU Open Data Portal is home to vital open data pertaining to EU policy domains. These policy domains include economy, employment, science, environment, and education. Around 70 EU institutions, organizations or departments such as Eurostat, the European Environment Agency, the Joint Research Centre and other European Commission Directorates-General and EU Agencies have made their datasets public and allowed access. These datasets have crossed the number of 11700 till date.

The portal enables easy access. You can easily search, explore, link, download and reuse the data through a catalog of common metadata. You can do so for your specific purposes. It could be commercial or non-commercial purposes. You can search the metadata catalog through an interactive search engine (Data tab) and SPARQL queries (Linked data tab).

By making use of this catalog, you can gain access to the data stored on the different websites of the EU institutions, agencies and organizations.

Five Thirty Eight

It is a great site for data-driven journalism and story-telling. It provides its various sources of data for a variety of sectors such as politics, sports, science, economics etc. You can download the data as well. When you access the data, you will come across a brief explanation regarding each dataset with respect to its source. You will also get to know what it stands for and how to use it.

In order to render this data user-friendly, it provides datasets in as simple, non-proprietary formats such as CSV files as possible. Needless to say, these formats can be easily accessed and processed by humans as well as machines. With the help of these datasets, you can create stories and visualizations as per your own requirements and preference.

U.S. Census Bureau

U.S. Census Bureau is the biggest statistical agency of the federal government. It stores and provides reliable facts and data regarding people, places, and economy of America. The Census Bureau considers its noble mission to extend its services as the most reliable provider of quality data.

Whether it is a federal, state, local or tribal government, all of them make use of census data for a variety of purposes. These governments use this data to determine the location of new housing and public facilities. They also make use of it at the time of examining the demographic characteristics of communities, states, and the USA.

This data is also made use of in planning of transportation systems and roadways. When it comes to deciding quotas and creating police and fire precincts, this data comes in handy. When governments create localized areas of elections, schools, utilities etc, they make use of this data. It is a practice to compile population information once a decade and this data are quite useful in accomplishing the same. There are various tools such as American Fact Finder, Census Data Explorer and Quick Facts which are useful in case you want to search, customize and visualize data.

For instance, Quick Facts alone contains statistics for all the states, counties, cities and even towns with a population of 5000 or more. Likewise, American Fact Finder can help you discover popular facts such as population, income etc. It provides information that is frequently requested.

The good thing is that you can search, interact with the data, get to know about popular statistics and see the related charts through Census Data Explorer. Moreover, you can also use visual tool to customize data on an interactive maps experience.

Data.gov

Data.gov is the treasure-house of US government's open data. It was only recently that the decision was made to make all government data available for free. When it was launched, there were only 47. There are now 180,000 datasets.

Why Data.gov is a great resource is because you can find data, tools, and resources that you can deploy for a variety of purposes. You can conduct your research, develop your web and mobile applications and even design data visualizations.

All you need to do is enter keywords in the search box and browse through types, tags, formats, groups, organization types, organizations, and categories. This will facilitate easy access to data or datasets that you need. Data.gov follows the Project Open Data Schema — a set of requisite fields (Title, Description, Tags, Last Update, Publisher, Contact Name, etc.) for every data set displayed on Data.gov.

DBpedia

As you know, Wikipedia is a great source of information. DBpedia aims at getting structured content from the valuable information that Wikipedia created. With DBpedia, you can semantically search and explore relationships and properties of Wikipedia resource.

There are around 4.58 million entities in the DBpedia dataset. 4.22 million are classified in ontology, including 1,445,000 persons, 735,000 places, 123,000 music albums, 87,000 films,

19,000 video games, 241,000 organizations, 251,000 species and 6,000 diseases. There are labels and abstracts for these entities in around 125 languages. There are 25.2 million links to images. There are 29.8 million links to external web pages. All you need to do in order to use DBpedia is write SPARQL queries against endpoint or by downloading their dumps. DBpedia has benefitted several enterprises, such as Apple (via Siri), Google (viaFreebase and Google Knowledge Graph), and IBM (via Watson), and particularly their respective prestigious projects associated with artificial intelligence.

Free Code Camp Open Data

It is an open source community. Why it matters is because it enables you to code, build pro bono projects after nonprofits and grab a job as a developer. In order to make this happen, the freeCodeCamp.org community makes available enormous amounts of data every month. They have turned it into open data. You will find a variety of things in this repository. You can find datasets, analysis of the same and even demos of projects based on the freeCodeCamp data.

You can also find links to external projects involving the freeCodeCamp data. It can help you with a diversity of projects and tasks that you may have in mind. Whether it is web analytics, social media analytics, social network analysis, education analysis, data visualization, data-driven web development or bots, the data offered by this community can extremely useful and effective.

Yelp Open Datasets

The Yelp dataset is basically a subset of nothing but our own businesses, reviews and user data for use in personal, educational and academic pursuits. There are 5,996,996 reviews, 188,593 businesses, 280,991 pictures and 10 metropolitan areas included in Yelp Open Datasets.

You can use them for different purposes. Since they are available as JSON files, you can use them in order to teach students about databases. You can use them to learn NLP or for sample production data while you understand how to design mobile apps. In this dataset, you will find each file composed of a single object type, one JSON- object per- line.

UNICEF Dataset

Since UNICEF concerns itself with a wide variety of critical issues, it has compiled relevant data on education, child labor, child disability, child mortality, maternal mortality, water and sanitation, low birth-weight, antenatal care, pneumonia, malaria, iodine deficiency disorder, female genital mutilation/cutting, and adolescents. UNICEF's open datasets published on the IATI Registry: http://www.iatiregistry.org/publisher/unicef has been extracted directly from UNICEF's operating system (VISION) and other data systems, and it reflects inputs made by individual UNICEF offices. The good thing is that there is a regular update when it comes to these datasets. Every month, the data is updated in order to make it more comprehensive, reliable and accurate. You can freely and easily access this data. In order to do so, you can download this data in CSV format. You can also preview sample data prior to downloading it. While anybody can explore and visualize UNICEF's datasets, there are three principal publishers:

Unicef's Aid Transparency Portal

You can far more easily access the datasets if you use this portal. It also includes details for each country that UNICEF works in.

- **Publisher d-portal :** It is, at the moment, in BETA. With this, portal, you can explore IATI data. You can search the information related to development activities, budgets etc. You can explore this information country-wise.
- **Publisher's data platform :** On this platform, you can easily access statistics, charts, and metrics on data accessed via the IATI Registry. If you click on the headers, you can also sort many of the tables that you see on the platform. You will also find many of the datasets in the platforms in machine-readable JSON format.

Kaggle

Kaggle is great because it promotes the use of different dataset publication formats. However, the better part is that it strongly recommends that the dataset publishers share their data in an accessible, non-proprietary format. The platform supports open and accessible data formats. It is important not just for access but also for whatever you want to do with this data. Therefore, Kaggle Dataset clearly defines the file formats which are recommended while sharing data. The unique thing about Kaggle datasets is that it is not just a data repository. Each dataset stands for a community that enables you to discuss data, find out public codes and techniques, and conceptualize your own projects in Kernels. CSV, JSON, SQLite, Archive, Big Query etc. are files types that Kaggle supports. You can find a variety of resources in order to start working on your open data project. The best part is that Kaggle allows you to publish and share datasets privately or publicly.

LODUM

It is the Open Data initiative of the University of Münster. Under this initiative, it is made possible for anyone to access any public information about the university in machine-readable formats. You can easily access and reuse it as per your needs. Open data about scientific artifacts and encoded as linked data is made available under this project. With the help of Linked Data, it is possible to share and use data, ontologies and various metadata standards. It is, in fact, envisaged that it will be the accepted standard for providing metadata, and the data itself on the Web. You can use SPARQL editor or SPARQL package of R to analyze data. SPARQL Package enables to connect to a SPARQL endpoint over HTTP, pose a SELECT query or an update query (LOAD, INSERT, DELETE).

UCI Machine Learning Repository

It serves as a comprehensive repository of databases, domain theories, and data generators that are used by the machine learning community for the empirical analysis of machine learning algorithms. In this repository, there are, at present, 463 datasets as a service to the machine learning community. The Center for Machine Learning and Intelligent Systems at the University of California, Irvine hosts and maintains it. David Aha had originally created it as a graduate student at UC Irvine. Since then, students, educators, and researchers all over the world make use of it as a reliable source of machine learning datasets.

How it works is that each dataset has its distinct webpage which enlists all the known details including any relevant publications that investigate it. You can download these datasets as ASCII files, often the useful CSV format. The details of datasets are summarized by aspects like attribute types, number of instances, number of attributes, and year published that can be sorted and searched.

1.10 DATA APIS

A Data API provides *API* access to data stored in a Data management system. APIs provide granular, per-record access to datasets and their component data files.

Limitations of APIs

Whilst Data APIs are in many ways more flexible than direct downloads they have disadvantages:

- APIs are much more costly and complex to create and maintain than direct download
- API queries are slow and limited in size because they run in real-time in memory. Thus, for bulk access e.g. of the entire dataset direct download is much faster and more efficient (downloading a 1GB CSV directly is easy and takes seconds but attempting to do so via the API may crash the server and be very slow).

Why Data APIs?

- **Data (pre)viewing**: reliably and richly (e.g. with querying, mapping etc). This makes the data much more accessible to non-technical users.
- **Visualization and analytics**: rich visualization and analytics may need a data API (because they need easily to query and aggregate parts of dataset).
- **Rich Data Exploration**: when exploring the data you will want to explore through a dataset quickly only pulling parts of the data and drilling down further as needed.
- **(Thin) Client applications**: with a data API third party users of the portal can build apps on top of the portal data easily and quickly (and without having to host the data themselves)

On the other side they provide support for:

- **Rapidly updating data e.g. timeseries**: if you are updating a dataset every minute or every second you want an append operation and don't want to store the whole file every update just to add a single record

- **Datasets stored as structured data by default** and which can therefore be updated in part, a few records at a time, rather than all at once (as with blob storage)

Domain Model

The functionality associated to the Data APIs can be divided in 6 areas:

1. **Descriptor**: metadata describing and specifying the API e.g. general metadata e.g. name, title, description, schema, and permissions
2. **Manager** for creating and editing APIs.

API

API for creating and editing Data API's descriptors (which triggers creation of storage and service endpoint)

1. **Service (read):** web API for accessing structured data (i.e. per record) with querying etc. *When we simply say "Data API" this is usually what we are talking about*
   - Custom API & Complex functions: e.g. aggregations, join
   - **Tracking & Analytics:** rate-limiting etc
   - **Write API:** usually secondary because of its limited performance vs bulk loading
   - Bulk export of query results especially large ones (or even export of the whole dataset in the case where the data is stored directly in the DataStore rather than the FileStore). This is an increasingly important feature a lower priority but if required it is substantive feature to implement.
2. **Data Loader**: bulk loading data into the system that powers the data API.
   - **Bulk Load:** bulk import of individual data files
   - Maybe includes some ETL => This takes us more into the data factory
3. **Storage (Structured)**: the underlying structured store for the data (and its layout). For example, Postgres and its table structure. This could be considered a separate component that the Data API uses or as part of the Data API – in some cases the store and API are completely wrapped together, e.g. Elastic Search is both a store and a rich Web API.

1.11 WEB SCRAPING

Web scraping is an automatic method to obtain large amounts of data from websites. Most of this data is unstructured data in an HTML format which is then converted into structured data in a spreadsheet or a database so that it can be used in various applications. There are many different ways to perform web scraping to obtain data from websites. These include using online services, particular API's or even creating your code for web scraping from scratch.

Many large websites, like Google, Twitter, Facebook, StackOverflow, etc. have API's that allow you to access their data in a structured format. This is the best option, but there are other sites that don't allow users to access large amounts of data in a structured form or they are simply not that technologically advanced. In that situation, it's best to use Web Scraping to scrape the website for data.

Web scraping requires two parts, namely the **crawler** and the **scraper**. The crawler is an artificial intelligence algorithm that browses the web to search for the particular data required by following the links across the internet. The scraper, on the other hand, is a specific tool created to extract data from the website. The design of the scraper can vary greatly according to the complexity and scope of the project so that it can quickly and accurately extract the data.

How Web Scrapers Work?

Web Scrapers can extract all the data on particular sites or the specific data that a user wants. Ideally, it's best if you specify the data you want so that the web scraper only extracts that data quickly. For example, you might want to scrape an Amazon page for the types of juicers available, but you might only want the data about the models of different juicers and not the customer reviews.

So, when a web scraper needs to scrape a site, first the URLs are provided. Then it loads all the HTML code for those sites and a more advanced scraper might even extract all the CSS and Javascript elements as well. Then the scraper obtains the required data from this HTML code and outputs this data in the format specified by the user. Mostly, this is in the form of an Excel spreadsheet or a CSV file, but the data can also be saved in other formats, such as a JSON file.

Different Types of Web Scrapers

Web Scrapers can be divided on the basis of many different criteria, including Self-built or Pre-built Web Scrapers, Browser extension or Software Web Scrapers, and Cloud or Local Web Scrapers. You can have **Self-built Web Scrapers** but that requires advanced knowledge of programming. And if you want more features in your Web Scrapper, then you need even more knowledge. On the other hand, pre-built **Web Scrapers** are previously created scrapers that you can download and run easily. These also have more advanced options that you can customize.

- **Browser extensions Web Scrapers** are extensions that can be added to your browser. These are easy to run as they are integrated with your browser, but at the same time, they are also limited because of this. Any advanced features that are outside the scope of your browser are impossible to run on Browser extension Web Scrapers. But **Software Web Scrapers** don't have these limitations as they can be downloaded and installed on your computer. These are more complex than Browser web scrapers, but they also have advanced features that are not limited by the scope of your browser.
- **Cloud Web Scrapers** run on the cloud, which is an off-site server mostly provided by the company that you buy the scraper from. These allow your computer to focus on other tasks as the computer resources are not required to scrape data from websites. **Local Web Scrapers**, on the other hand, run on your computer using local resources. So, if the Web scrapers require more CPU or RAM, then your computer will become slow and not be able to perform other tasks.

Why Is Python a Popular Programming Language for Web Scraping?

Python seems to be in fashion these days! It is the most popular language for web scraping as it can handle most of the processes easily. It also has a variety of libraries that were created specifically for Web Scraping. **Scrapy** is a very popular open-source web crawling framework that is written in Python. It is ideal for web scraping as well as extracting data using APIs. **Beautiful soup** is another Python library that is highly suitable for Web Scraping. It creates a parse tree that can be used to extract data from HTML on a website. Beautiful soup also has multiple features for navigation, searching, and modifying these parse trees.

What is Web Scraping Used for?

Web Scraping has multiple applications across various industries. Let's check out some of these now!

Price Monitoring

Web Scraping can be used by companies to scrap the product data for their products and competing products as well to see how it impacts their pricing strategies. Companies can use this data to fix the optimal pricing for their products so that they can obtain maximum revenue.

Market Research

Web scraping can be used for market research by companies. High-quality web scraped data obtained in large volumes can be very helpful for companies in analyzing consumer trends and understanding which direction the company should move in the future.

News Monitoring

Web scraping news sites can provide detailed reports on the current news to a company. This is even more essential for companies that are frequently in the news or that depend on daily news for their day-to-day functioning. After all, news reports can make or break a company in a single day!

Sentiment Analysis

If companies want to understand the general sentiment for their products among their consumers, then Sentiment Analysis is a must. Companies can use web scraping to collect data from social media websites such as Facebook and Twitter as to what the general sentiment about their products is. This will help them in creating products that people desire and moving ahead of their competition.

Email Marketing

Companies can also use Web scraping for email marketing. They can collect Email ID's from various sites using web scraping and then send bulk promotional and marketing Emails to all the people owning these Email ID's.

1.12 RELATIONAL DATABASE ACCESS (QUERIES) TO PROCESS/ ACCESS DATA

Using a query makes it easier to view, add, delete, or change data in your Access database. Some other reasons for using queries:

- Find specific quickly data by filtering on specific criteria (conditions)

- Calculate or summarize data
- Automate data management tasks, such as reviewing the most current data on a recurring basis.
- Queries help you find and work with your data
- Create a select query
- Create a parameter query
- Create a totals query
- Create a crosstab query
- Create a make table query
- Create an append query
- Create an update query
- Create a delete query

Queries Help to Find and Work with your Data

In a well-designed database, the data that you want to present through a form or report is usually located in multiple tables. A query can pull the information from various tables and assemble it for display in the form or report. A query can either be a request for data results from your database or for action on the data, or for both. A query can give you an answer to a simple question, perform calculations, combine data from different tables, add, change, or delete data from a database. Since queries are so versatile, there are many types of queries and you would create a type of query based on the task.

Major	query	Us
Select		To retrieve data from a table or make calculations
Actio		Add, change, or delete data. Each task has a specific type of action query. Action queries available in Access web apps.

Create a Select Query

If you want to review data from only certain fields in a table, or review data from multiple tables simultaneously or maybe just see the data based on certain criteria, a select query type would be your choice.

Review Data from Select Fields

For example, if your database has a table with a lot of information about products and you want to review a list of products and their prices, here's how you'd create a select query to return just the product names and the respective price:

- Open the database and on the **Create** tab, click **Query Design.**
- On the **Tables** tab, double-click the **Products** table.
- In the Products table, let's say that you have Product Name and List Price fields. Double- click the **Product Name** and **List Price** to add these fields to the query design grid.
- On the **Design** tab, click **Run**. The query runs, and displays a list of products and their prices.

Review Data from Multiple Related Tables Simultaneously

For example, if you have a database for a store that sells food items and you want to review orders for customers who live in a particular city. Say that the data about orders and data about customers are stored in two tables named Customers and Orders respectively. If each table has a Customer ID field, which forms the basis of a one-to- many relationship between the two tables. You can create a query that returns orders for customers in a particular city, for example, Las Vegas, by using the following procedure:

1. Open the database. On the **Create** tab, in the **Query** group, click **Query Design**.
2. On the **Tables** tab, double-click **Customers** and **Orders**.

   Note the line (called a join) that connects the ID field in the Customers table and the Customer ID field in the Orders table. This line shows the relationship between the two tables.
3. In the Customers table, double-click **Company** and **City** to add these fields to the query design grid.
4. In the query design grid, in the **City** column, clear the check box in the **Show** row.
5. In the **Criteria** row of the **City** column, type **Las Vegas**.

   Clearing the **Show** check box prevents the query from displaying the city in its results, and typing **Las Vegas** in the **Criteria** row specifies that you want to see only records where the value of the City field is Las Vegas. In this case, the query returns only the customers that are located in Las Vegas. You don't need to display a field to use it with a criterion.
6. In the Orders table, double-click **Order ID** and **Order Date** to add these fields to the next two columns of the query design grid.
7. On the **Design** tab, in the **Results** group, click **Run**. The query runs, and then displays a list of orders for customers in Las Vegas.
8. Press CTRL+S to save the query.

Create a Parameter Query

If you frequently want to run variations of a particular query, consider using a parameter query. When you run a parameter query, the query prompts you for field values, and then uses the values that you supply to create criteria for your query.

Continuing from the previous example where you learnt to create a select query that returns orders for customers located in Las Vegas, you can modify the select query to prompt you to specify the city each time that you run the query. To follow along, open the database that you created in the previous example:

1. In the Navigation Pane, right-click the query named Orders by City (that you created in the previous section), and then click Design View on the shortcut menu.
2. In the query design grid, in the Criteria row of the City column, delete Las Vegas, and then type [For what city?].

   The string [For what city?] is your parameter prompt. The square brackets indicate that you want the query to ask for input, and the text (in this case, For what city?) is the question that the parameter prompt displays.
3. Select the check box in the Show row of the City column, so that the query results will display the city.

4. On the Design tab, in the Results group, click Run. The query prompts you to enter a value for City.
5. Type New York, and then press ENTER to see orders for customers in New York.

   What if you don't know what values you can specify? You can use wildcard characters as part of the prompt:
6. On the Home tab, in the Views group, click View, and then click Design View.
7. In the query design grid, in the Criteria row of the City column, type Like [For what city?]&"*".

   In this parameter prompt, the **Like** keyword, the ampersand (**&**), and the asterisk (*) enclosed in quotation marks allow the user to type a combination of characters, including wildcard characters, to return a variety of results. For example, if the user types *, the query returns all cities; if the user types **L**, the query returns all cities that start with the letter "L;" and if the user types ***s***, the query returns all cities that contain the letter "s."
8. On the **Design** tab, in the **Results** group, click **Run**, and at the query prompt, type **New**, and press ENTER.

   The query runs, and then displays orders for customers in New York.

Display Summarized or Aggregate Data

When you use tables to record transactions or store regularly occurring numeric data, it is useful to be able to review that data in aggregate, such as sums or averages. In Access, you can add a Totals row to a datasheet. Total row is a row at the bottom of the datasheet that can display a running total or other aggregate value.

1. Run the Product Subtotals query you created earlier, and leave the results open in Datasheet view.
2. On the **Home** tab, click **Totals**. A new row appears at the bottom of the datasheet, with the word **Total** in the first column.
3. Click the cell in the last row of the datasheet named **Total**.
4. Click the arrow to view the available aggregate functions. Because the column contains text data, there are only two choices: **None** and **Count**.
5. Select **Count**. The content of the cell changes from **Total** to a count of the column values.
6. Click the adjoining cell (the second column). Note that an arrow appears in the cell.
7. Click the arrow, and then click **Sum**. The field displays a sum of the column values.
8. Leave the query open in the Datasheet view.

Create a Make Table Query

You can use a make-table query to create a new table from data that is stored in other tables.

For example, suppose that you want to send data for Chicago orders to a Chicago business partner who uses Access to prepare reports. Instead of sending all your order data, you want to restrict the data that you send to data specific to Chicago orders. You can build a select query that contains Chicago order data, and then use the select query to create the new table by using the following procedure:

1. Open the example database from the previous example.

   To run a make-table query, you may need to enable the database content.
2. On the **Create** tab, in the **Query** group, click **Query Design**.
3. Double-click **Order Details** and **Orders**.
4. In the **Orders** table, double-click **Customer ID** and **Ship City** to add these fields to the design grid.
5. In the **Order Details** table, double-click **Order ID**, **Product ID**, **Quantity**, **Unit Price**, and **Discount** to add these fields to the design grid.
6. In the **Ship City** column of the design grid, clear the box in the **Show** row. In the **Criteria** row, type **'Chicago'** (include the single quotation marks). Verify the query results before you use them to create the table.
7. On the **Design** tab, in the **Results** group, click **Run**.
8. Press Ctrl + S to save the query.
9. In the **Query Name** box, type **Chicago Orders Query**, and then click **OK**.
10. On the **Home** tab, in the **Views** group, click **View**, and then click **Design View**.
11. On the **Design** tab, in the **Query Type** group, click **Make Table**.
12. In the **Make Table** dialog box, in the **Table Name** box, type **Chicago Orders**, and then click **OK**.
13. On the **Design** tab, in the **Results** group, click **Run**.
14. In the confirmation dialog box, click **Yes**, and see the new table displayed in the Navigation Pane.

Create an Append Query

You can use an append query to retrieve data from one or more tables and add that data to another table.

For example, suppose that you created a table to share with a Chicago business associate, but you realize that the associate also works with clients in the Milwaukee area. You want to add rows that contain Milwaukee area data to the table before you share the table with your associate. You can add Milwaukee area data to the Chicago Orders table by using the following procedure:

1. Open the query named "Chicago Orders Query" you created earlier in Design view.
2. On the **Design** tab, in the **Query Type** group, click **Append**. The **Append** dialog box opens.
3. In the **Append** dialog box, click the arrow in the **Table Name** box, select **Chicago Orders** from the drop-down list, and then click **OK**.
4. In the design grid, in the **Criteria** row of the Ship City column, delete 'Chicago', and then type **'Milwaukee'**.
5. In the **Append To** row, select the appropriate field for each column.

   In this example, the **Append To** row values should match the **Field** row values, but that is not required for append queries to work.
6. On the **Design** tab, in the **Results** group, click **Run**.

UNIT 2

Data Processing and Preparation

2.1 DATA MUNGING

What is Data Munging?

Data wrangling, or data munging, is the initial process of refining raw data into content or formats better suited for consumption by downstream systems and users. The term 'Mung' was coined in the late 1960s as a somewhat derogatory term for actions and transformations that progressively degrade a dataset. It quickly became tied to the backronym "Mash Until No Good" (or, recursively, "Mung Until No Good").

But as data practitioners' diversity, expertise, and specialization grew in the internet age, 'munging' and 'wrangling' became more useful generic terms, analogously to 'coding' for software engineers.

With the rise of cloud computing and storage, and more sophisticated analytics, these terms evolved further, and today refer specifically to the initial collection, preparation, and refinement of raw data.

The Data Munging Process

With the wide variety of verticals, use cases, types of users, and systems utilizing enterprise data today, the specifics of munging can take on myriad forms.

- **Data exploration**: Munging usually begins with data exploration. Whether an analyst is merely peeking at completely new data in initial data analysis (IDA), or a data scientist begins the search for novel associations in existing records in exploratory data analysis (EDA), munging always begins with some degree of data discovery.
- **Data transformation**: Once a sense of the raw data's contents and structure have been established, it must be transformed to new formats appropriate for downstream processing.

  This step involves the pure data scientist, for example, un-nesting hierarchical JSON data, demoralizing disparate tables so relevant information can be accessed from one place, or reshaping and aggregating time series data to the dimensions and spans of interest.
- **Data enrichment**: Optionally, once data is ready for consumption, data mungers might choose to perform additional enrichment steps. This involves finding external sources of information to expand the scope or content of existing records. For example, using an open-source weather dataset to add daily temperature to an ice cream shop's sales figures.

- **Data validation:** The final, perhaps most important, munging step is validation. At this point, the data is ready to be used, but certain common-sense or sanity checks are critical if one wishes to trust the processed data. This step allows users to discover typos, incorrect mappings, problems with transformation steps, and even the rare corruption caused by computational failure or error.

The most basic munging operations can be performed in generic tools like Excel or Tableau —from searching for typos to using pivot tables, or the occasional informational visualization and simple macro. But for regular mungers and wranglers, a more flexible, powerful programming language is far more effective.

Python is often lauded as the most flexible popular programming language, which is no exception when it comes to data munging. With one of the largest collections of third-party libraries, especially rich data processing and analysis tools like Pandas, NumPy, and SciPy, Python simplifies many complex data-munging tasks. Pandas, in particular, is one of the fastest-growing and best-supported data-munging libraries, while still only a tiny part of the massive Python ecosystem.

Python is also easier to learn than many other languages thanks to simpler, more intuitive formatting, as well as a focus on legible English-language-adjacent syntax. Python's wide applicability, rich libraries, and online support, new practitioners will additionally find the language useful far beyond data processing use cases, everywhere from web development to workflow automation. Data science is the study of data. Like biological sciences is a study of biology, physical sciences, it's the study of physical reactions. Data is real, data has real properties, and we need to study them if we're going to work on them. Data Science involves data and some signs.

2.2 DATA WRANGLING

Data wrangling is the process of cleaning and unifying messy and complex data sets for easy access and analysis. With the amount of data and data sources rapidly growing and expanding, it is becoming increasingly essential for large amounts of available data to be organized for analysis. This process typically includes manually converting and mapping data from one raw form into another format to allow for more convenient consumption and organization of the data.

The Goals of Data Wrangling

- Reveal a "deeper intelligence" by gathering data from multiple sources
- Provide accurate, actionable data in the hands of business analysts in a timely matter
- Reduce the time spent collecting and organizing unruly data before it can be utilized
- Enable data scientists and analysts to focus on the analysis of data, rather than the wrangling
- Drive better decision-making skills by senior leaders in an organization

Key Steps to Data Wrangling

- **Data Acquisition**: Identify and obtain access to the data within your sources.
- **Joining Data**: Combine the edited data for further use and analysis.

- **Data Cleansing**: Redesign the data into a usable and functional format and correct/remove any bad data.

Package Managers are tools that help you manage the dependencies for your project. A dependency is a code that is required for your program to function properly. These often come in the form of packages. Packages can also have their dependencies. Managing all these dependencies can be hard because packages may require specific versions of their dependencies. It's easy to break something by modifying dependencies manually.

Data Science is kind a blended with various tools, algorithms, and machine learning principles. Most simply, it involves obtaining meaningful information or insights from structured or unstructured data through a process of analyzing, programming and business skills. It is a field containing many elements like mathematics, statistics, computer science, etc. Those who are good at these respective fields with enough knowledge of the domain in which you are willing to work can call themselves as Data Scientist. It's not an easy thing to do but not impossible too. You need to start from data, it's visualization, programming, formulation, development, and deployment of your model. In the future, there will be great hype for data scientist jobs. Taking in that mind, be ready to prepare yourself to fit in this world.

2.3 DATA VISUALIZATION BASICS

Data visualization is the graphical representation of information and data. By using visual elements like charts, graphs, and maps, data visualization tools provide an accessible way to see and understand trends, outliers, and patterns in data. In the world of Big Data, data visualization tools and technologies are essential to analyze massive amounts of information and make data-driven decisions.

The Advantages and Benefits of Good Data Visualization

Our eyes are drawn to colors and patterns. We can quickly identify red from blue, square from circle. Our culture is visual, including everything from art and advertisements to TV and movies. Data visualization is another form of visual art that grabs our interest and keeps our eyes on the message. When we see a chart, we quickly see trends and outliers. Ifwe can see something, we internalize it quickly. It's storytelling with a purpose.

As the "age of Big Data" kicks into high-gear, visualization is an increasingly key tool to make sense of the trillions of rows of data generated every day. Data visualization helps to tell stories by curating data into a form easier to understand, highlighting the trends and outliers. A good visualization tells a story, removing the noise from data and highlighting the useful information. However, it's not simply as easy as just dressing up a graph to make it look better or slapping on the "info" part of info graphic. Effective data visualization is a delicate balancing act between form and function. The plainest graph could be too boring to catch any notice or it could not tell a powerful point; the most stunning visualization could utterly fail at conveying the right message or it could speak volumes. The data and the visuals need to work together, and there's an art to combining great analysis with great storytelling.

2.4 PLYR PACKAGE IN R PROGRAMMING

The dplyr package in R Programming Language is a structure of data manipulation that provides a uniform set of verbs, helping to resolve the most frequent data manipulation hurdles. The dplyr Package in R performs the steps given below quicker and in an easier fashion: By limiting the choices the focus can now be more on data manipulation difficulties. There are uncomplicated "verbs", functions present for tackling every common data manipulation and the thoughts can be translated into code faster. There are valuable backends and hence waiting time for the computer reduces.

Melting and Casting In R

Melting and Casting are of interesting aspects in R programming to change the shape of the data and further, get the desired shape. R programming language has many methods to reshape the data using the reshape package. melt() and cast() are the functions that efficiently reshape the data. There are many packages in R that require data reshaping. Each data is specified in multiplier owes of a data frame with different details in each row and this type of format of data is known as long format.

Melting in R

Melting in R programming is done to organize the data. It is performed using the melt() function which takes dataset and column values that has to be kept constant. Using melt(), the data frame is converted into a long format and stretches the data frame.

Syntax: melt(data,na.rm=FALSE,value.name="value")

Parameters: Data: represents dataset that has to be reshaped na.rm: if TRUE, removes NA values from dataset value.name: represents the name of a variable used to store values

Example

- Required library for ships dataset install.packages("MASS")
- Required for melt() and cast() function install.packages("reshape2") install.packages("reshape")
- Loading the libraries library (MASS) library(reshape2) library(reshape)
- Create data frame n <- c(1, 1, 2, 2)

```
time<-c(1,2,1,2)
x<-c(6,3,2,5)
y<-c(1,4,6,9)
df <-data.frame (n,time,x,y)
#Original data frame   cat("Original data frame:\n") print(df)
#Organize data w.r.t. n and time molten.data <- melt(df, id = c("n","time"))
cat("\nAfter melting data frame:\n") print(molten.data)
```

Output

Original data frame: n time x y

11	161
21	234
32	126
42	259

After melting data frame: n time variable value

11	1	x	6
21	2	x	3
32	1	x	2
42	2	x	5
51	1	y	1
61	2	y	4
72	1	y	6
82	2	y	9

Casting in R

Casting in R programming is used to reshape the molten data using the cast() function which takes an aggregate function and formula to aggregate the data accordingly. This function is used to convert long-format data back into some aggregated form of data based on the formula in the cast() function.

Syntax: `cast(data,formula,fun.aggregate)`

Parameters

data: represents a dataset

formula: represents the form in which data has to be reshaped fun. aggregate: represents aggregate function

Example

```
# Print recasted dataset using cast() function cast.data <-
cast(molten.data, n~variable, sum)
print(cast.data) cat("\n")
time.cast<-cast(molten.data,time~variable, mean) print(time.cast)
```

Output

nxy

1195

22715

timexy

1 143.5

2 246.5

2.5 TABLEAU

Tableau is a leading data visualization tool used for data analysis and business intelligence. Gartner's Magic Quadrant classified Tableau as a leader for analytics and business intelligence. This Tableau has lot of features including how to create different charts and graphs, in addition to visualizing data through reports and dashboards in Tableau to derive meaningful insights.

What is Tableau?

Tableau is an excellent data visualization and business intelligence tool used for reporting and analyzing vast volumes of data. It is an American company that started in 2003—in June 2019, Sales force acquired Tableau. It helps users create different charts, graphs, maps, dashboards, and stories for visualizing and analyzing data, to help in making business decisions.

Tableau has a lot of unique, exciting features that make it one of the most popular tools in business intelligence (BI). Let's learn more about some of the essential Tableau Desktop features. Now that we know what is tableau exactly, let us understand some of its salient features.

Tableau Features

Tableau supports powerful data discovery and exploration that enables users to answer important questions in seconds No prior programming knowledge is needed; users without relevant experience can start immediately with creating visualizations using Tableau, It can connect to several data sources that other BI tools do not support.

Tableau enables users to create reports by joining and blending different datasets. Tableau Server supports a centralized location to manage all published data sources within an organization.

Installing Tableau Desktop

Knowing what is tableau is the first step, however, how to install it follows right after. The following are the steps for downloading Tableau Desktop:

Click on the Products Download and Release Notes page and select the version you want to download.

Tableau Version

Select the DOWNLOAD TABLEAU DESKTOP version option and select your operating system.

Download Tableau

Once you have downloaded the file, go ahead and install it.

Launch Tableau Desktop, and it will show you the Tableau registration form, which is where you can register and activate your product.

Activate Tableau

Enter your product key, or sign in to Tableau Server or Tableau Online to activate your Tableau license. Upon successful activation, you can start using Tableau Desktop.

Tableau provides us with various services according to our business needs Tableau Desktop, Tableau Public, and Tableau Online, all these offer Data Visual Creation. The choice of Tableau depends upon the type of work.

Getting Started with Data Visualization using Tableau

Once Tableau is installed in the system, let's see some real-world Data Visualization using Tableau.

Load Data in Tableau

- Global superstore data is used for analysis
- This link will take you to a page where you may download the dataset.

Y11

	I	S	M	N	D	P	O	B	S	T	U	V	W	S
1	Country	Postal Cod	Market	Region	Product-IL	Catagory	Sub Cakeg	Product N	Sales	Quantity	Discount	Profff	Shippiae	Order Prio
2	Untted State	10024	US	East	TEC-AC-10	Technologa	Acessoria	Plantronics	2309.65	8	0	722 L815	953.57	Critical
3	Ausfraiia		APAC	Oceania	FUR-1R-15	Furniture	Chairs	Novnnea Ei	3705.95	9	0.1	289 725	973.80	Critical
4	Australla		EU	Oceania	TEC-PH 10	Furniture	Phones	Nokia Snia	3061 32	5	0.1	309.416	891.16	High
3	Germany		Aftica	Cenical	FEC-TA1-4	Technologa	Phones	Motorola !	252 95	8	0.1	23	837.21	Medium
6	Sanagal		Africa	Atrica	TEC-TA-10	Technologa	Chairs	Sharp Wirt	2892.3	8	0	311.33	809.09	Critical
7	New Zealand		Africa	Oceania	FUR-TA-19	Furniture	Tables	Chromeraf	3344 08	4	0.1	388.185	838.84	High
8	New Sealand		Africa	Oceania	FUR-TA-10	Furniture	Tables	Chromcraf	3241.00	13	0	758.79	857.83	Low
9	United State	85923	US	South	OFF-SU-10	Office Supa	Furniture	Canon FA	316.73	9	0.3	1316 74	839.57	Low
19	Unfted State	28097	US	North	OFE-SU-10	Office Supa	Tables	Cloronos.FF	3237 79	4	0.1	1897 3031	833.98	Critical
1L	Auttraiia	21100	US	South	OFE-SU-10	Furniture	Tables	Chromcraf	5188.4	6	0	648.81	830.77	High
17	New Zealand		EMBA	Central Asia	COS-CS-10	Office Supa	Appliance	Motoroia E	6701.5	5	0	537.81	839.50	High
13	india		LATAM	South	COS-CS-10	Office Supa	Phones	Canon F4	454.05	4	0	634.72	830.20	Low
14	France		EU	Central Asia	Vidar	Furniture	Tables	Brother Re	1869 7	13	0	1078.12	880.54	Critical
15	India		APAC	South	OFF-SU-10	Office Supa	Furniture	Logitet Bai	2546.5	9	0.1	154.343	830 77	Critical
16	Saud Africa	45820	US	North	APP-IO-10	Office Supa	Appiiance	Canon F4	518.73	4	0	3378.55	725.88	Low
17	India		EU	South	Kitshengid	Speakers	Phones	Lagiteck St	5734.5	6	0	620.21	815.79	Critical
18	France		China	North	Hon Comp	Computer	Tables	Motorisa E	452 35	5	0	319.25	819.84	High
15	Saudl Arrabia		EMBA	South	Hon Comp	Camputer	Appliance	Ardimlerri	6026.6	4	0	280.44	820.25	Low
2J	India	60510	US	Central Asia	Hon Comp	Computer	Tables	Kitchenaid	5124.8	14	0	1728.12	824.54	Critical
21	France		UR	South	APP PH-10	Office Supa	Furniture	Hon Comp	2740.6	5	0.1	188.642	756 79	Critical
22	Ecuader		APAC	North	Hon Comp	Furniture	Tables	Hon Comp	50610	4	0	760.81	775.57	Critical
23	El Salvador		US	North	Hon Comp	Cumputer	Tables	Kitchenaid	5278.7	4	0	509.33	723.58	Critical
21	Serador		Abasa	North	Lecro Conf	Furniture	Tables	Hon Comp	1713.5	2	0	720.36	725.57	Critical

Orders Returns People

***Figure 2.1:** Sample data set*

The downloaded file is a zip file that contains an excel that looks like the given picture below:

- Now we have an excel file and Tableau installed let's load the dataset into Tableau.
- Tableau also gives us some flexibility to create new columns, rename, split, edit alias, join tables, some preprocessing before loading the data into Tableau.
- The below image will demonstrate to you how to load data and perform some preprocessing. Tableau supports various data formats which can be loaded by choosing those options.
- Under a file we see various options to load data from the local directory and under to a server, we see options to load data from cloud servers.
- For loading CSV files we select Text file options, for excel and SQL files we choose their respective options

Connect Tableaut to the Data File

- To open the application, click the Tableau icon on your desktop (or in your Start menu).
- In the Connect panel at the left side of the Start page, click the Excel link under the "To a File" heading to the open file selection option.
- Using the files election box, select the Excel worksheet that you want to open, and then click the Open button to continue

- Select the Orders sheet from the navigation menu on the left and drag it on to the Drag Sheets Here area, as shown in the above gif.
- After loading we can perform data cleaning, data preprocessing, and feature extraction to some extent.

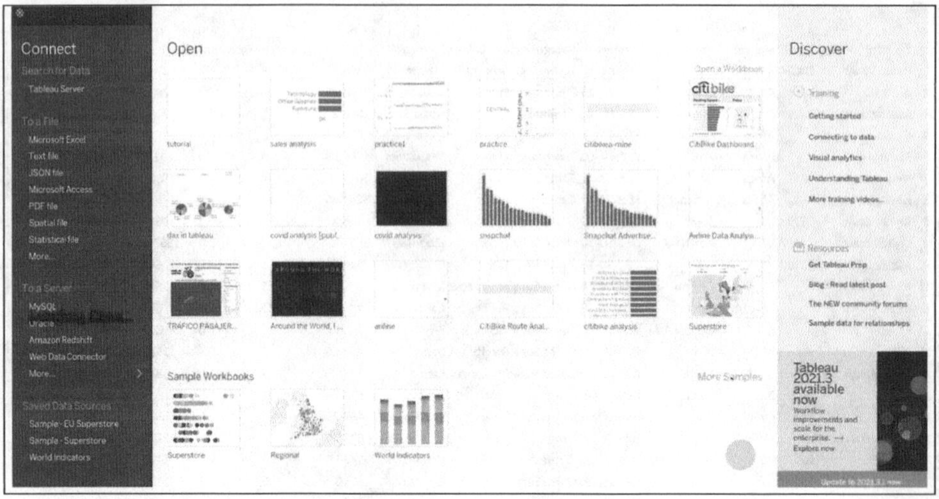

***Figure 2.2:** Tableau Screen*

Understanding different Sections in Tableau

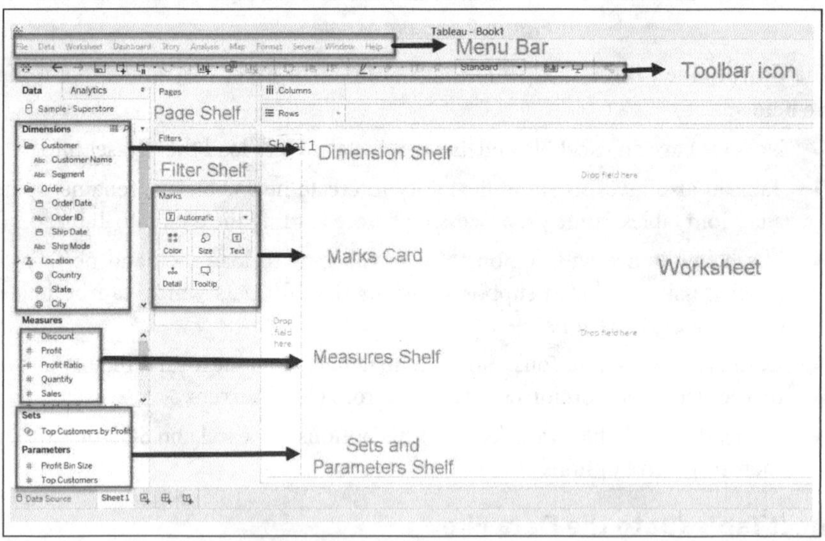

***Figure 2.3:** Tableau Workspace*

- Tableau loaded with global-superstore data and now we can see Tableau work-page.
- Tableau work-page consist of different section. Let's understand them first before plotting our graphs
- **Menu Bar:** Here you'll find various commands such as File, Data, and Format.

- **Toolbar Icon:** The toolbar contains a number of buttons that enable you to perform various tasks with a click, such as Save, Undo, and New Worksheet.
- **Dimension Shelf:** This shelf contains all the categories columns under it. example: categories, segments, gender, name, etc
- **Measure Shelf:** This shelf contains all numerical columns under it like profit, total sales, discount, etc
- **Page Shelf:** This shelf is used for joining pages and create animations. we will come on it later
- **Filter Shelf:** You can choose which data to include and exclude using the Filters shelf, for example, you might want to analyze the profit for each customer segment, but only for certain shipping containers and delivery times. You may make a view like this by putting fields on the Filters tier.
- **Marks Card:** The visualization can be designed using the Marks card. The markings card can be used to change the data components of the visualization, such as color, size, shape, path, label, and tooltip.

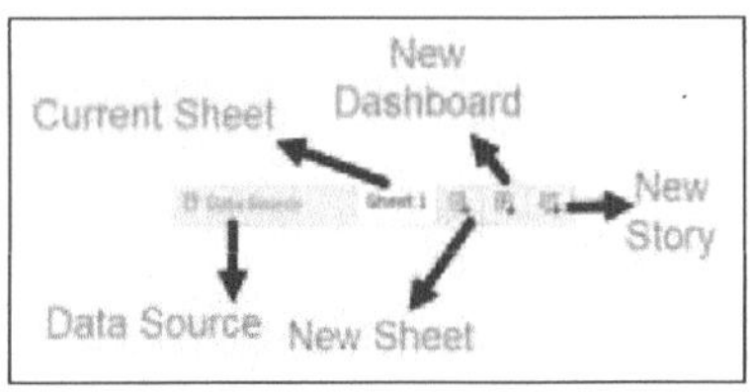

Figure 2.4: *Tableau Taskbar*

- **Worksheet:** In the workbook, the worksheet is where the real visualization may be seen. The worksheet contains information about the visual's design and functionality.
- **Data Source:** Using Data Source we can add new data, modify, and remove data.
- **Current Sheet:** The current sheets are those sheets that we have created and to those, we can give some names.
- **New Sheet:** If we want to create a new worksheet (blank canvas) we can do using this tab.
- **New Dashboard:** This button is used to create a dashboard canvas.
- **New Storyboard:** It is used to create a new story.

Creating Visuals in Tableau

Real data visualization using Tableau- Tableau supports the following data types:

- **Boolean:** True and false can be stored in this data type.
- **Date/Date time:** This data type can help in leveraging Tableau's default date hierarchy behavior when applied to valid date or Date Time fields.
- **Number:** These are values that are numeric. Values can be integers or floating-point numbers (numbers with decimals).
- **String:** This is a sequence of characters encased in single or double quotation marks.
- **Geo location:** These are values that we need to plot maps.

Follow These Steps

- Drag the dimension and measure in row and column input field and it will automatically suggest a graph best fitted on data.
- You can change the graph by clicking on the Show me button and selecting whichever graph you want.
- You can also remove the axis just by dragging and dropping them under the marks card (remove field).
- **Show Me:** When you click this label, a palette appears, giving your apid access to many options for showing the selected types of fields. The palette changes depending on the fields in the worksheet you've selected or are active.

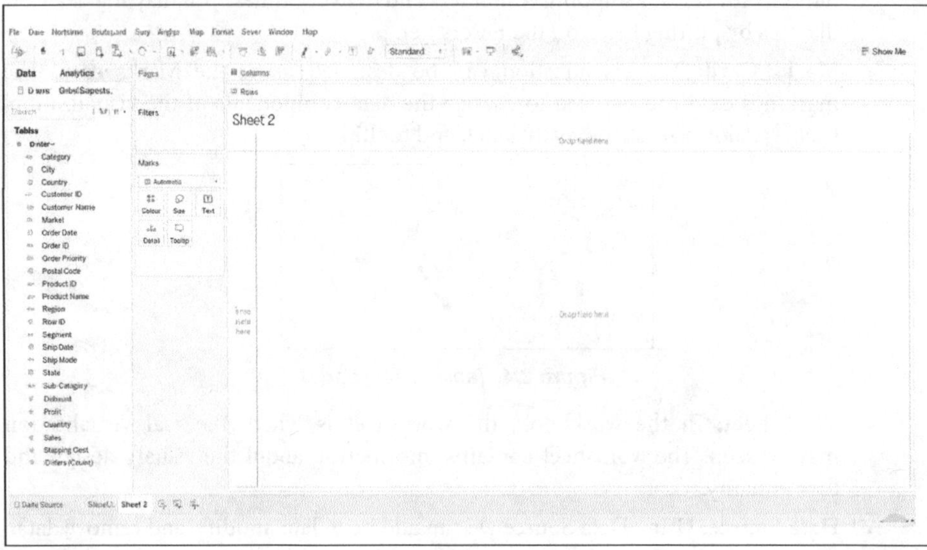

Figure 2.5

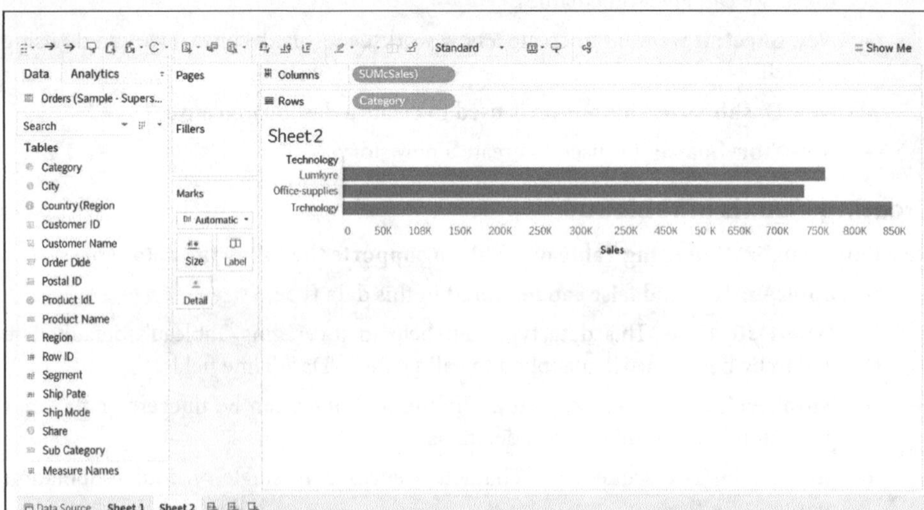

***Figure 2.6:** Visuals in Tableau*

From the above image, you might have observed that the default aggregation on the measure is sum but you can change the aggregation to sum, avg, min, max, etc, you can also customize the axis name, orientation, size, show-hide axis as shown in the above image. Create a hierarchy

Data Hierarchies in Tableau

The hierarchy in Tableau is an arrangement where entities are presented at various levels. So, there's an entity or dimension under which there are further entities present as levels. In Tableau, we can create hierarchies by bringing one dimension as a level under the principle dimension.

To Create a Hierarchy

- In the Data pane, drag a field and drop it directly on top of another field.
- Note: When you want to create a hierarchy from a field inside a folder, right-click (control-click on a Mac) the field and then select Create Hierarchy.
- When prompted, enter a name for the hierarchy and click OK.
- Drag additional fields into the hierarchy as needed. You can also re-order fields in the hierarchy by dragging them to a new position.

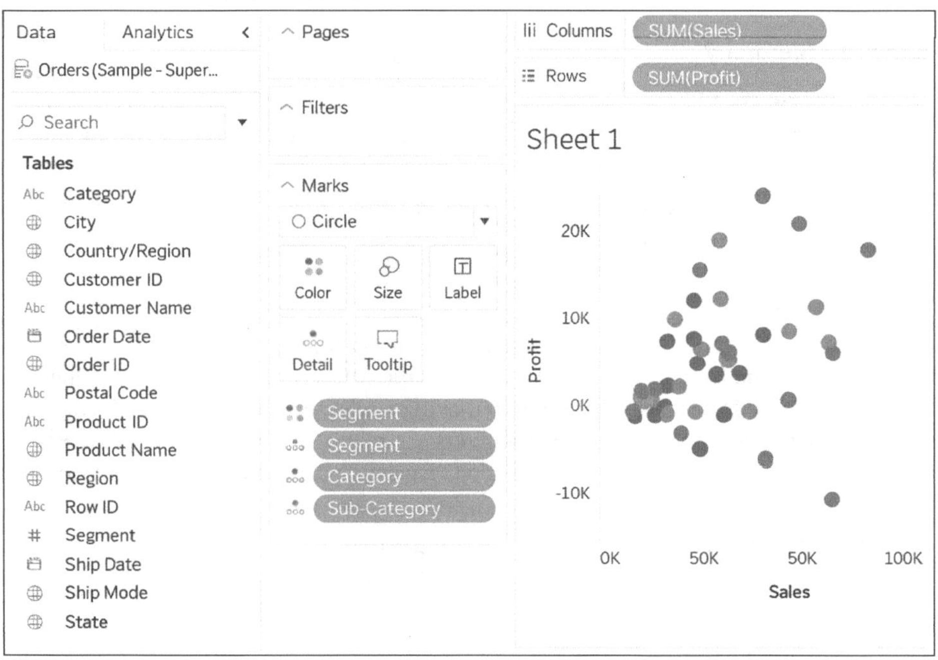

Figure 2.7: *Hierarchy Creation*

Drill Up or Down in a Hierarchy

- When you add a field from a hierarchy to the visualization, you can quickly drill up or down in the hierarchy to add or subtract more levels of detail.
- To drill up or down in the hierarchy in Tableau Desktop or web authoring:
- In the visualization, click the +or- icon on the hierarchy field.

- When you are editing or viewing the visualization on the web, you have the option of clicking the + or - icon next to a field label.

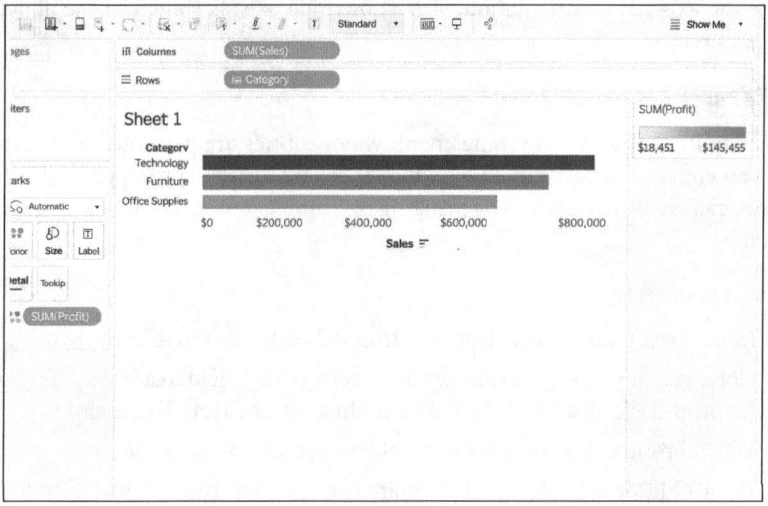

Figure 2.8: *Hierarchy Modification*

Remove a Hierarchy

- **To remove a hierarchy:**
- In the Data pane, right-click (control-click on a Mac) the hierarchy and select Remove Hierarchy.
- The fields in the hierarchy are removed from the hierarchy and the hierarchy disappears from the Data pane.

Filters in Tableau

Filters in a tableau can be used to organize data based on predefined conditions and use them for data visualization. Such ability to filter large datasets in the Business Intelligence tool helps prepare for analysis, including removing irrelevant data records, reducing data sizes for faster processing, and more. The filters are required to highlight any underlying insights that can be derived from the data upon visualizing in a readable, actionable format.

Tableau performs actions on your view in a very specific order; this is called the Order of Operations. Filters are executed in the following order:

- Extract filters
- Data source filters
- Context filters
- Filters on dimensions (whether on the Filters shelf or in filter cards in the view)
- Filters on measures (whether on the Filters shelf or in filter cards in the view)

After creating some plots, you might want to use different filters, to do so follow these steps:

- On the filter shelf, you can drag any measure or dimension whichever you want to apply a filter on.

- By dropping the field a box will appear, now you can select any particular category, or top-n rows according to measure values or you can write some rules to select top rows or by using some parameters.
- Now click on Show Filter after selecting the filter.
- Apply multiple filters; to do so you will need to add previous filters into context by clickingonaddtocontexthereContextFilterisaTableaufilterthatisappliedbeforeall other filters.
- You can choose different options standard, fit width, fit height, entire view from the toolbar in order to fit the visualization into the worksheet.

Groups in Tableau

Create a group to combine related members in a field. For example, if you are working with a view that shows average test scores by major, you might want to group certain majors to create major categories. English and History might be combined into a group called Liberal Arts Majors, while Biology and Physics might be grouped as Science Majors.

Groups are useful for correcting data err ors (e.g., combining CA, Calif., and California Into one data point) as well as answering "what if" type questions (e.g., combined the East and West regions?).

Create a Group

There are multiple ways to create a group. You can create a group from a field in the Data pane, or by selecting data in the view and then clicking the group icon.

Create a Group by Selecting the View

In the view, select one or more data points, and then, on the tool tip that appears, click the group icon.

Note: You can also select the group icon on the toolbar at the top of the workspace.

If there are multiple levels of detail in the view, you must select a level to group the members. You can select to group all dimensions, or just one The data which is Raw, original, and extracted directly from the official sources is known as primary data. This type of is collected directly by performing techniques such as questionnaires, interviews, and surveys. The data collected must be according to the demand and requirements of the target audience on which analysis is per for it would be a burden in the data processing.

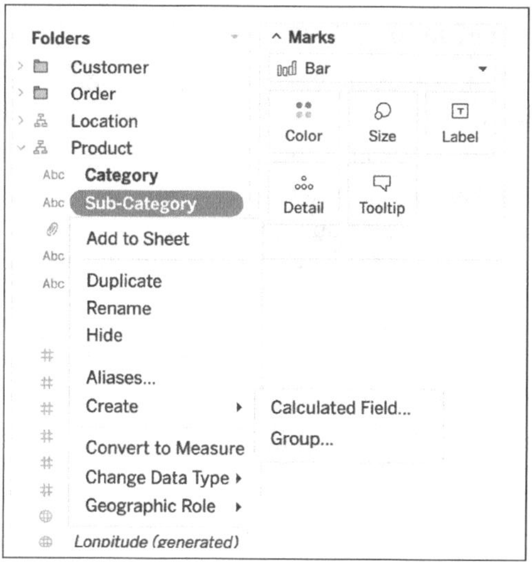

Figure 2.9

Create a group from a field in the Data pane and select several members that you wnt to group and then click Group.

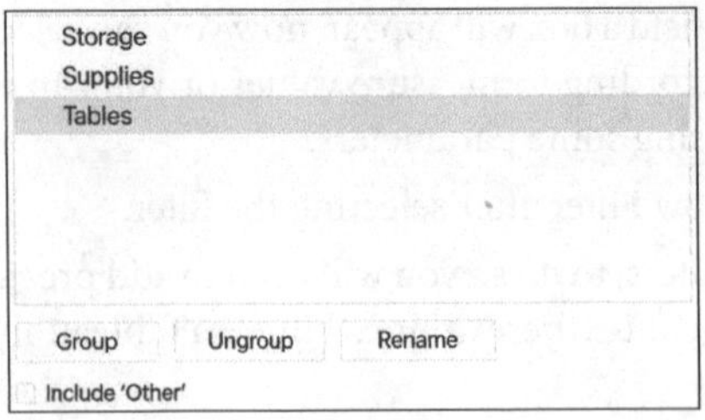

Figure 2.10: *Group Creation*

The selected members are combined into a single group. A default name is created using the combined member names.

To Rename the Group, Select it the List and Click Rename

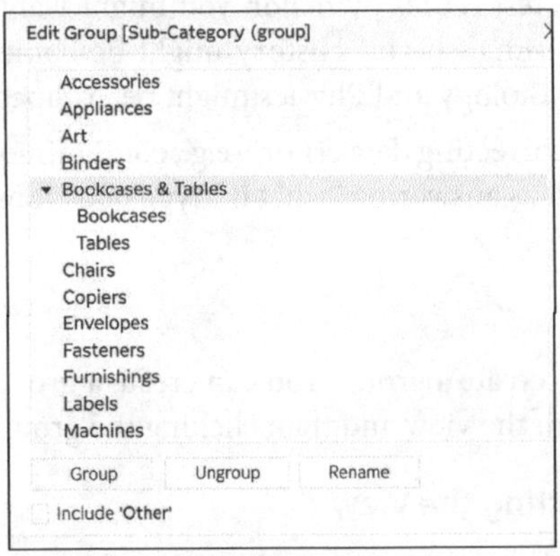

Figure 2.11: *Renaming Group*

Include an Other Group

When you create groups in Tableau, you have the option to group all remaining, or non-grouped members in another group.

The Include Other option is useful for highlighting certain groups or comparing specific groups against everything else. For example, if have a view that shows the sales versus profit product category, you might want to highlight the high and low-performing categories in the view, and group all the other categories into an "Other" group.

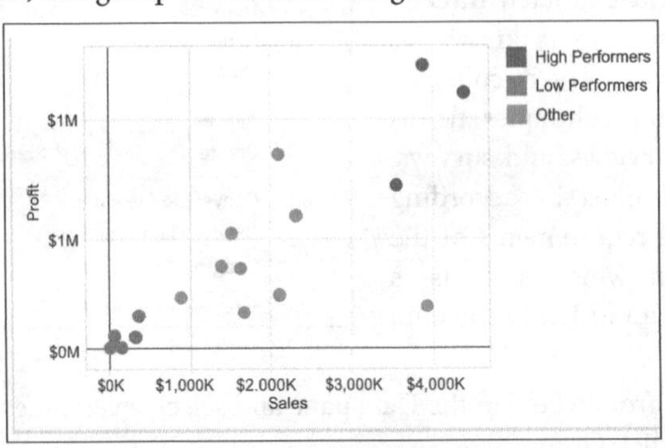

Figure 2.12

To Include Another Group

In the Data pane, right-click the group field and select Edit Group.

In the Edit Group dialog box, select Include 'Other'.

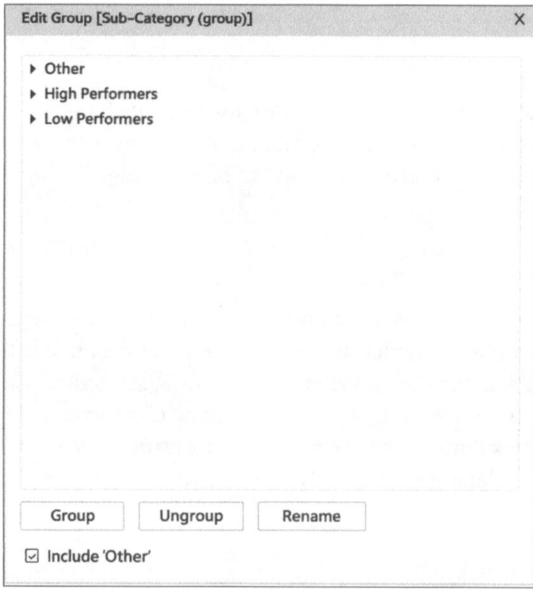

Figure 2.13: *Adding non Group members*

Edit a Group

After you have created a group field, you can add and remove members from the groups, create new groups, change the default group names, and change the name of the grouped field. You can make some changes directly in the view, and others through the Edit Group dialog box.

To Add Members to an Existing Group

- In the Data pane, right-click the group field, and then click Edit Group
- In the Edit Group dialog box, the group you want.
- Click OK.
- To remove members from an existing group:
- In the Data pane, right-click the group field, and then click Edit Group.
- In the Edit Group dialog box, select one or more members, and then click Ungroup.
- The members are removed from the current group. If you have another group, the members are added to it.
- Click OK.

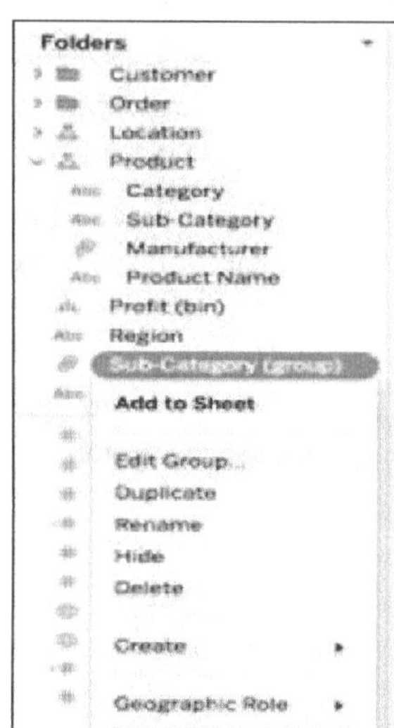

Figure 2.14: *Adding members in a existing group*

- To create a new group in a group field:
- In the Data pane, right-click the group field, and then click Edit Group.
- In the Edit Group dialog box, select one or more members, and then click Group.
- Click OK

Sets Tableau

Tableau Sets are custom fields used to hold the subset of data based on a given condition. In real-time, you can create a set by selecting members from the list in a visualization. You can also do the same by writing custom Conditions or Selecting the Top/Bottom few records in a Measure

You can use sets to compare and ask questions about a subset of data. Sets are custom fields that define a subset of data based on some conditions.

You can make sets more dynamic and interactive by using them in Set Actions. Set actions to let your audience interact directly with a viz or dashboard to control aspects of their analysis. When someone selects marks in the view, set actions can change the values in a set. In addition to a Set Action, you can also allow users to change the membership of a set by using a filter-like interface known as a Set Control, which makes it easy for you to designate inputs into calculations that drive interactive analysis. For details, see Show a set control in the view.

Create a Dynamic Set

There are two types of sets: dynamic sets and fixed sets. The members of a dynamic set change when the underlying data changes. Dynamic sets can only be based on a single dimension.

To Create a Dynamic Set

In the Data pane, right-click a dimension and select Create>Set.

In the create set dialog box configure your set, you can configure your set using the following tabs

- **General:** Use the General tab to select one or more values that will be considered when computing the set.

  You can alternatively select the Use all option to always consider all members even when new members are added or removed.

- **Condition:** Use the Condition tab to define rules that determine which members to include in the set.

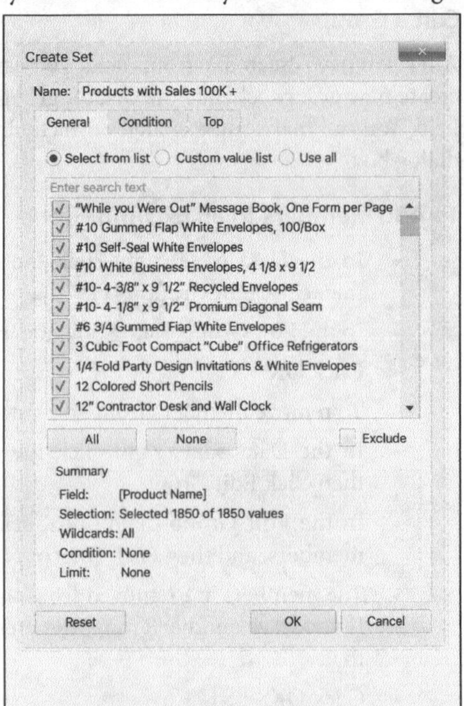

Figure 2.15: *Creating a set*

For example, you might specify a condition that is based on total sales that only includes products with sales over $100,000.

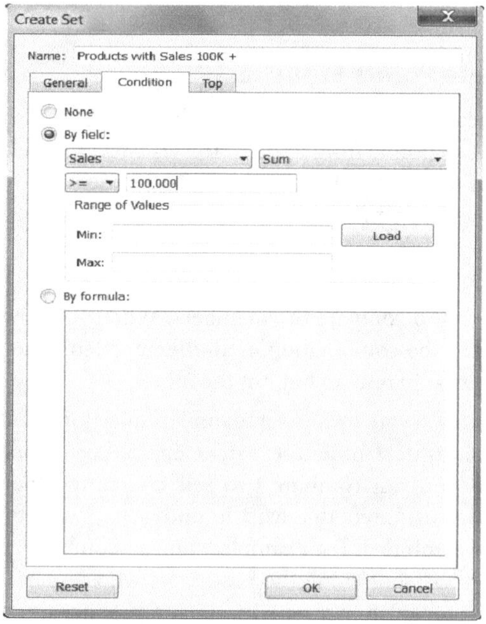

Figure 2.16: *Creating a set*

Top: Use the Top tab to define limits on what members to include in the set.

For example, you might specify a limit that is based on total sales that only includes the top products based on their sales.

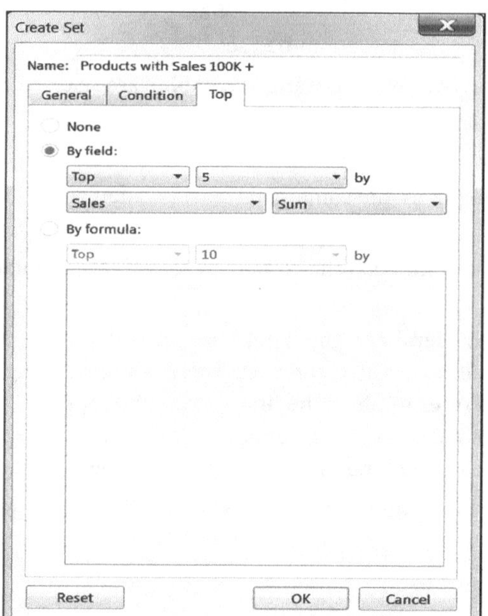

Figure 2.17: *Creating a set*

When finished, click OK.

The new set is added to the bottom of the data pane under the Sets section. A section indicates the field as a set

Add or Remove Data Points From Sets

If you create a set of specific data points, you can add more data to or subtract gata fom the set. To add or remove data points from a set. In the visualization, select the data points you want add or remove. In the tooltip that appears. Click the sets drop-down menu icon, and then select Add to [Name] or remove from [set],

Combine Sets

You can combine two sets to compare the members. When you combine sets you create a new set containing either the combination of all members, just the members that exist in both, or members that exist in one set but not the other.

Combining sets allows you to answer complex questions and compare cohorts of your data. For example, to determine the percentage of customers who purchased both last year and this year, you can combine two sets containing the customers from each year and return only the customers that exist in both sets. Two sets must be based on the same dimensions to be combined. For example, you can combine a set containing the top customers with another set containing the customers who purchased last year. However, you cannot combine the top customer set with the top product set.

To Combine Sets

In the Data pane, under Sets, select the sets you want to combine. Right-click the sets and select Create Combined Set.

In the Create Set dialog box, do the following

- Type a name for the new combined set.
- Verify that the two sets you want to combine are selected in the two drop-down menus.

Elect one of the following options for how to combine the sets:

All Members in Both Sets-the combined set will contain all of the members from both sets.

Shared Members in Both Sets- the combined set will only contain members that exist in both sets.

Except for Shared Members: the combined set will contain all members from the specified set that don't exist in the second set. These options are equivalent to subtracting one set from another. For example, if the first set contains Apples, Oranges, and Pears and the second set contains pears and nuts; combining the first set except the shared members would contain just Apples and Oranges. Pears is removed because it exist in the second set.

Optionally specify a character that will separate the members if the sets represent multiple dimensions.

When finished, click OK.

To switch a set to list the individual members:

In the visualization workspace, right-click the set and select Show Members in Set

Calculated Fields

Calculated fields allow you to create new data from data that already exists in your data source. When you create a calculated field, you are essentially creating a new field (or column) in your data source, the values or members of which are determined by a calculation that you control.

Step1: Create the Calculated Field

- In a worksheet in Tableau, select Analysis>Create Calculated Field.
- In the Calculation Edit or that opens, give the calculated field a name.
- In this example, the calculated field is called Profit Ratio.

Step2: Enter a formula

In the Calculation Editor, enter a formula.

- This example uses the following formula:

SUM([Profit])/SUM([Sales])

Formulas use a combination of functions, fields, and operators. To learn more about creating formulas in Tableau, see Formatting Calculations in Tableau (Link opens in a new window) and Functions in Tableau (Link opens in a new window).

When finished, click OK.

The new calculated field is added to the Data pane. If the new field computes quantitative data, it is added to Measures. If it computes qualitative data, It is added to Dimensions

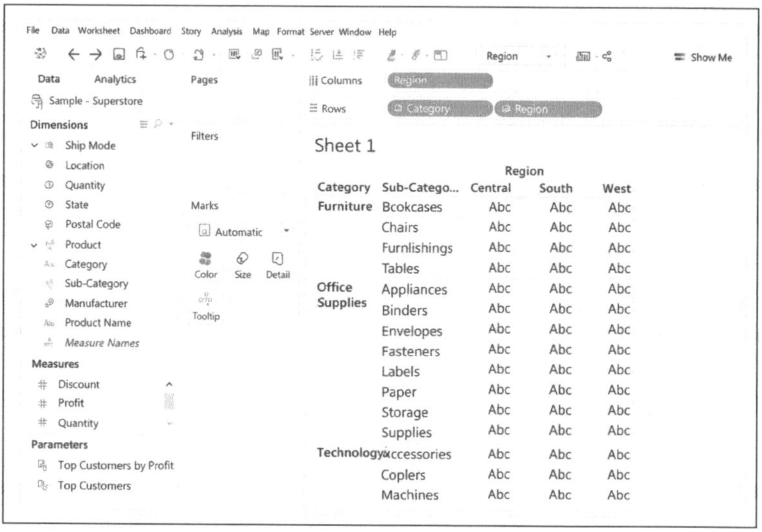

***Figure 2.18:** Creating Calculated field*

Map Based Visualizations

If you want to analyze your data geographically, you can plot your data on a map in Tableau. This topic explains why and when you should put your data on a map visualization. It also describes some of the types of maps you can create in Tableau, with links to topics that demonstrate how to create each one.

Why Put your Data on A Map?

There are many reasons to put your data on a map. Perhaps you have some location data in your data source? Or maybe you think a map could really make your data pop? Both of those are good enough reasons to create a map visualization, but it's important to keep in mind that maps, like any other type of visualization, serve a particular purpose: they answer spatial questions.

You make a map in Tableau because you have spatial questions, and you need to use a map to understand the trends or patterns in your data.

When Should you Use a Map to Represent your Data?

If you have a spatial question, a map view might be a great way to answer it. However, that might not always be the case.

Take, for example, the first question from the list above: Which state has the most farmers markets?

If you had a data source with a list of farmers' markets per state, you might create a map view like the one below. Can you easily tell the difference between New York and California? Which one has more farmers' markets?

What Types of Maps Can you Build in Tableau?

With Tableau, you can create the following common map types:

- Proportional symbol maps
- Choropleth maps (filled maps)
- Point distribution maps
- Heatmaps (density maps)
- Flow maps (path maps)
- Spider maps (origin-destination maps)
- Proportional symbol maps

1. Proportional Symbol Maps

Proportional symbol maps are great for showing quantitative data for individual locations. For example, you can plot earthquakes around the world and size them by magnitude.

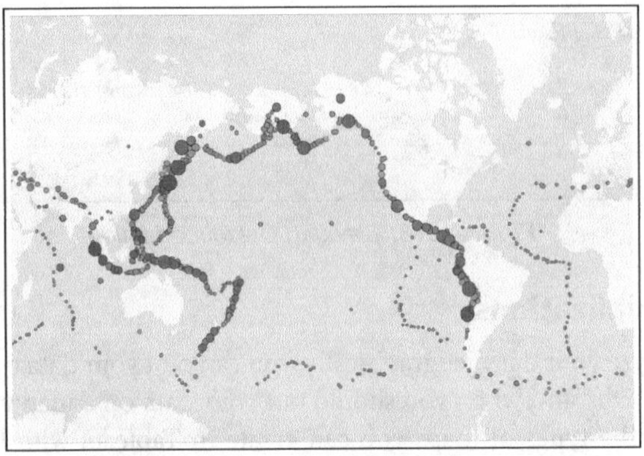

Figure 2.19: *Proportional Symbol maps*

2. Choropleth Maps

Choropleth maps (filled maps), also known as filled maps in Tableau, are great for showing ratio data. For example, if you want to see obesity rates for every county across the United States, you might consider creating a choropleth map to see if you can spot any spatial trends.

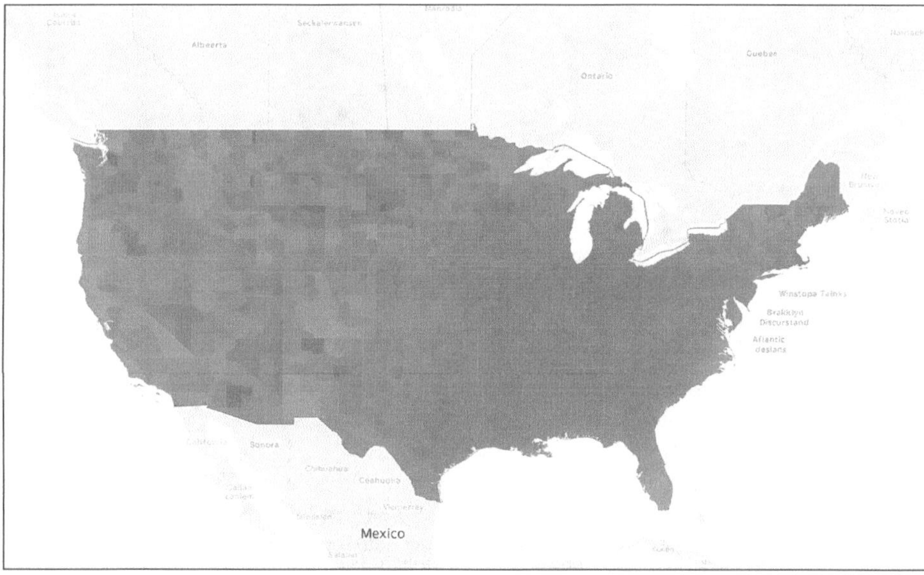

Figure 2.20: *Choropleth maps*

3. Heatmaps (Density Maps)

Heatmaps, or density maps, can be used when you want to show a trend for visual clusters of data. For example, if you want to find out which areas of Manhattan have the most taxi pickups, you can create a density map to see which areas are most popular.

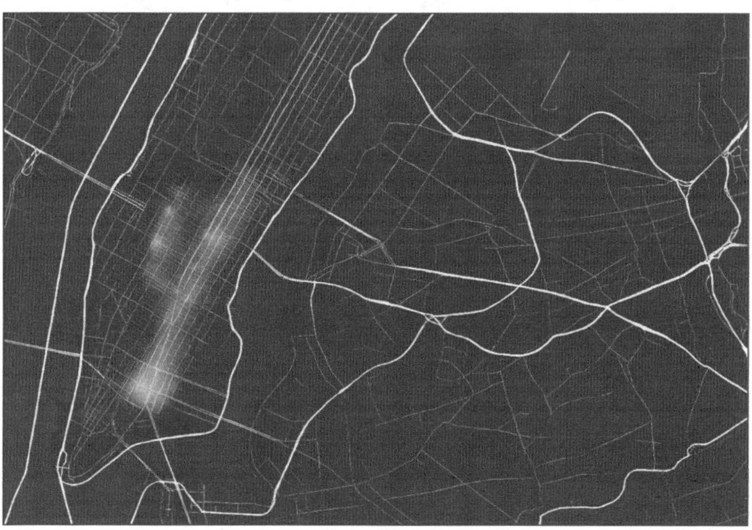

Figure 2.21: *Heat maps*

4. Flow Maps (Path Maps)

You can use flow maps to connect paths across a map to see where something went over time. For example, you can track the paths of major storms across the world over some time.

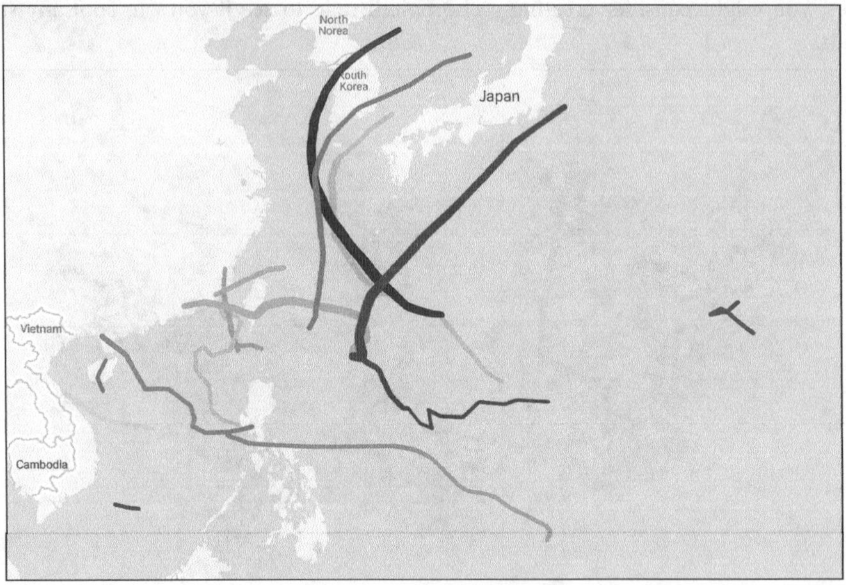

Figure 2.22: *Flow maps*

6. Spider Maps (Origin-Destination Maps)

You can use a spider map to show how an origin location and one or more destination locations interact. For example, you can connect paths between metro stations plot them on a map, or you can track bike share rides from an origin to one or more destinations.

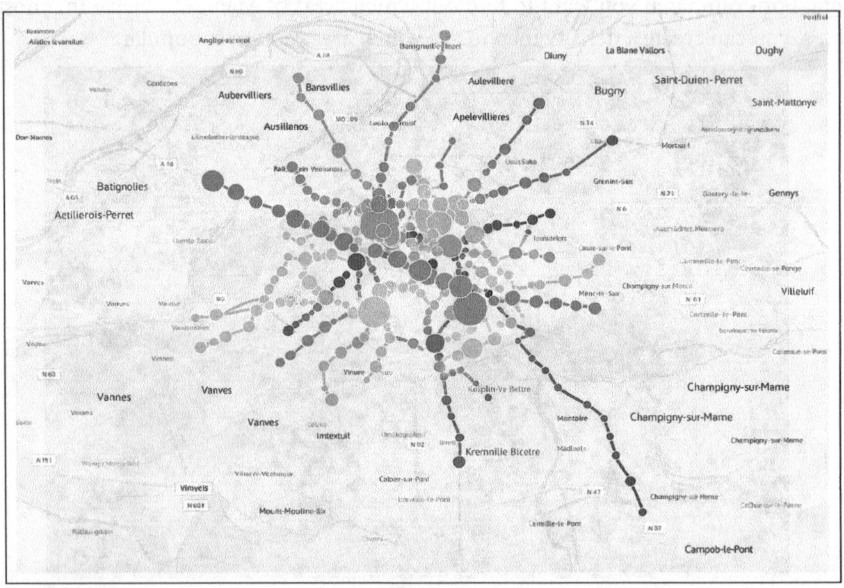

Figure 2.23: *Spider maps*

Build Interactive Dashboards

You've created four worksheets, and they're communicating important information that needs to be known. Now you need a way to show the negative profits in Tennessee, North Carolina, and Florida and explain some of the reasons why profits are low. To do this, you can use dashboards to display multiple worksheets at once, and—if you want—make them interact with one another.

Set up your Dashboard

You want to emphasize that certain items sold in certain places are doing poorly. Your bar graph view of profit and your map view demonstrates this point nicely.

- Click the New Dashboard button.
- The New Dashboard icon
- In the Dashboard pane on the left, you'll see the sheets that you created. Drag Sales in the South to your empty dashboard.
- Drag Profit Map to your dashboard, and drop it on top of the Sales in the South view.

Your view will update to look like this:

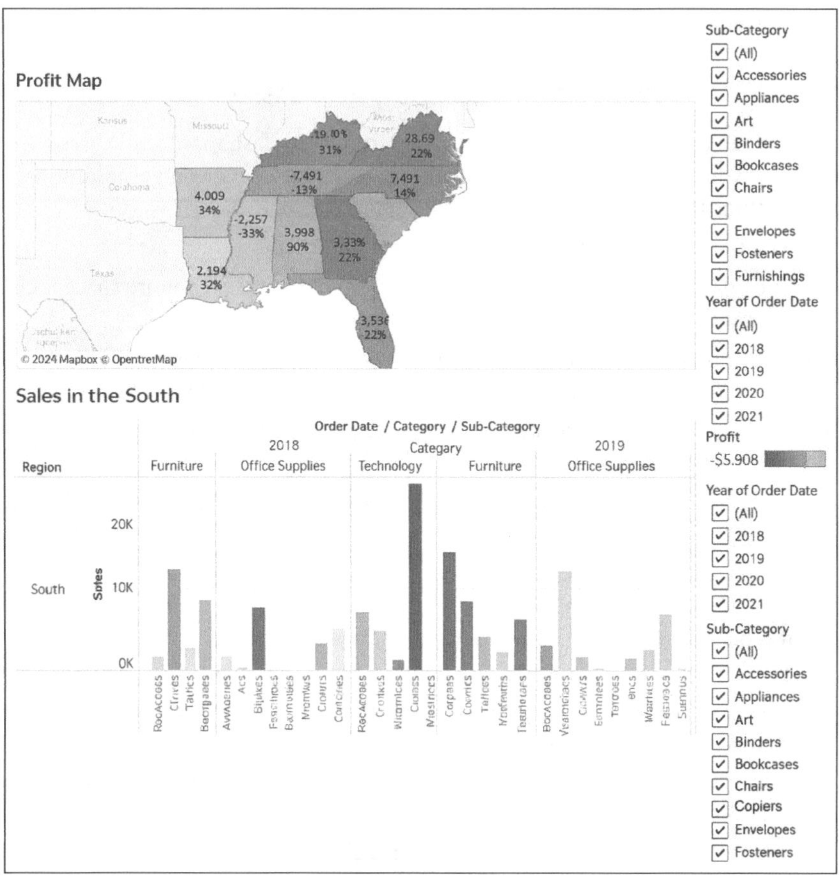

Figure 2.24: *Dashboard Creation*

Arrange Your Dashboard

It's not easy to see details for each item under Sub-Category from your Sales in the South bar chart. Also, because we have the main view, we probably don't need the South region column in Sales in the South, On Sales in the South, right-click in the column area under the Region column header, and clear the Show header.

Repeat this process for the **Category** row header.

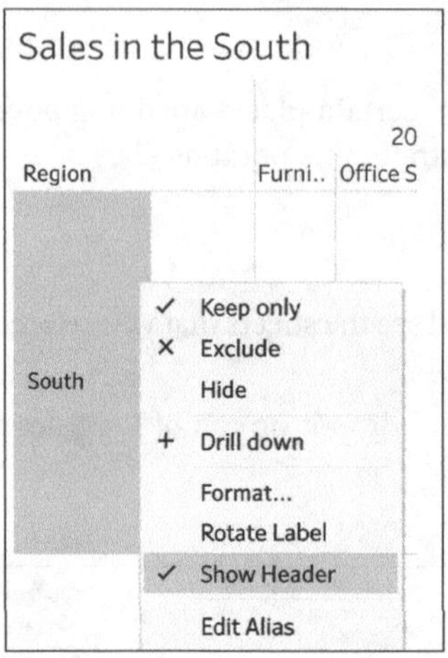

Figure 2.25

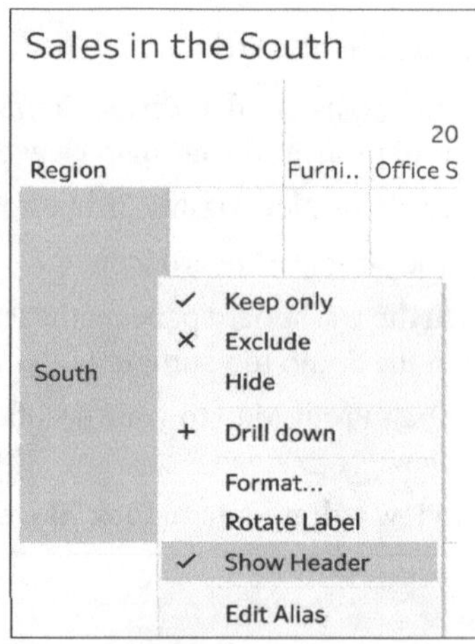

Figure 2.26: *Dashboard Modification*

Now hidden unnecessary columns and rows from your dashboard while preserving the breakdown of your data. The extra space makes it easier to see data on your dashboard, but let's freshen things up even more.

- Right-click the Profit Map title and select Hide Title.
- The title Profit Map is hidden from the dashboard and even more space is created. Repeat this step for the Sales in the South view title.
- Select the first Sub-Category filter card on the right side of your view, and at the top of the card, click the Remove icon The Remove from Dashboard icon.
- Repeat this step for the second Sub-Category filter card and one of the year-of-order date filter cards.
- Click on the Profit color legend and drag it from the right to below Sales in the South.
- Finally, select the remaining Year of Order Date filter, click its drop-down arrow, and then select Floating. Move to the white space in the map view. In this example, it is placed just off the East Coast, in the Atlantic Ocean.
- Try selecting different years on the Year of Order Date filter. Your data is quickly filtered to show that state performance varies year by year. That's nice, but it could be made even easier to compare.
- Click the drop-down arrow at the top of the Year of Order Date filter, and select Single Value (Slider).
- Select Profit Map in the dashboard, and click the Use as filter icon (The Use as Filter icon in the upper right corner).

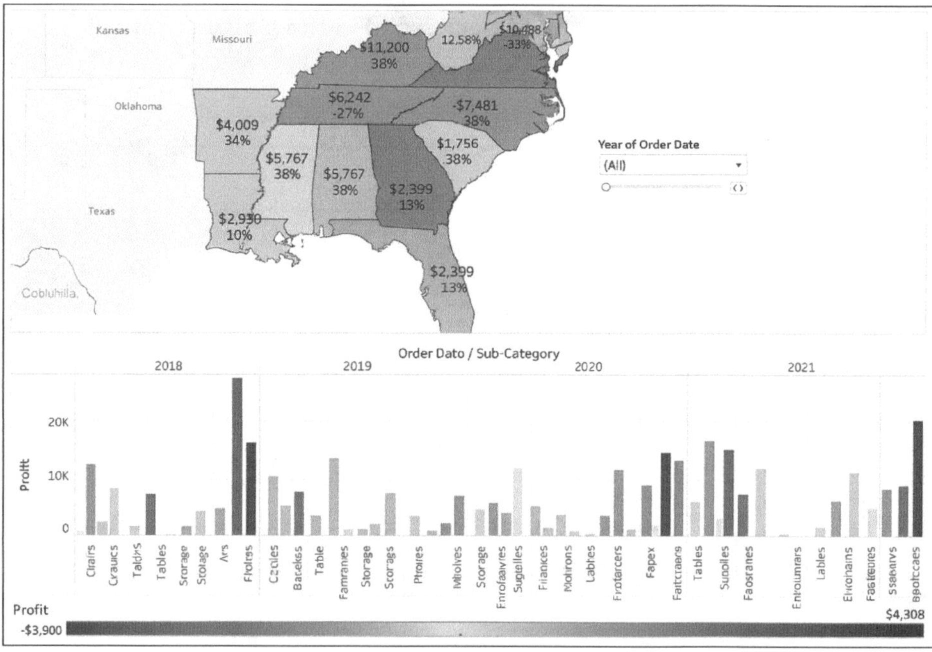

Figure 2.27: Profit Map

- Select a state within the Southern region of the map.
- The Sales in the South bar chart automatically updates to show just the sub-category sales in the selected state. You can quickly see which sub-categories are profitable.
- Click an area of the map other than the colored Southern states to clear your selection. You also want viewers to be able to see the change in profits based on the order date.
- Select the Year of an Order Date filter, click it drop-down arrow, and select Apply to Worksheets > Selected Worksheets.
- In the Apply Filter to Worksheets dialog box, select All in the dashboard, and then click OK. This option tells Table to apply the filter to all worksheets in the dashboard that use this same data source

2.6 DATA STORIES

In Tableau, a story is a sequence of visualizations that work together to convey information

You can create stories to tell a data narrative, provide context, demonstrate decisions related to outcomes or to simply make a compelling case

A story is a sheet, so the methods you use to create, name, and manage worksheets and dashboards also apply to stories (for more details, see Workbooks and Sheets). At the same time, a story is also a collection of sheets, arranged in a sequence. Each sheet in a story is called a story point.

When you share a story —for example, by publishing a workbook to Tableau Public, Tableau Server, or Tableau Online—users can interact with the story to reveal new findings or ask new questions about the data.

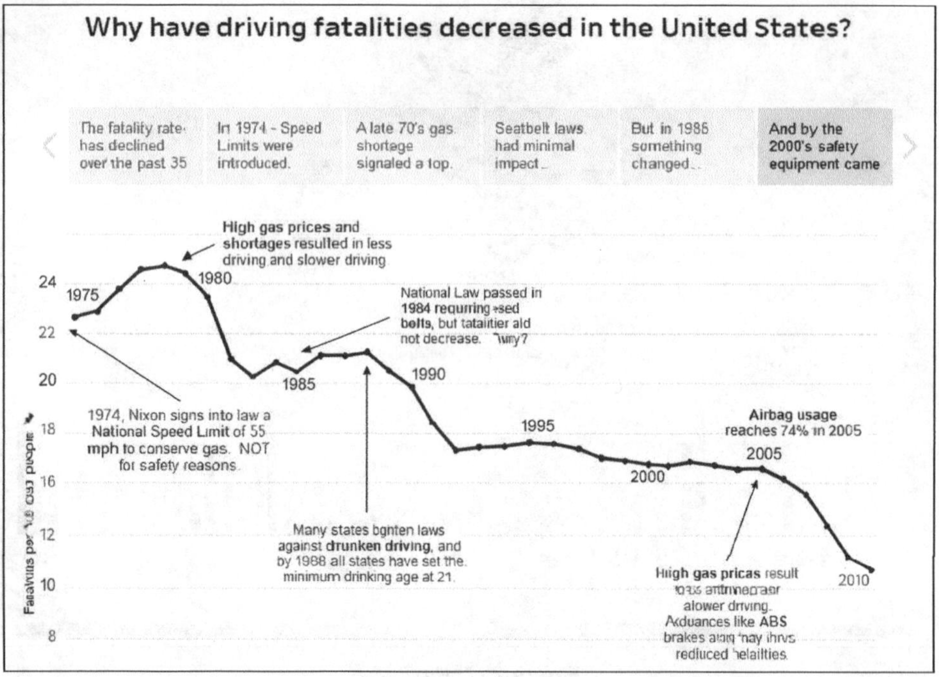

Figure 2.28: *Arrangement of Worksheets*

UNIT 3

Data Quality and Transformation

3.1 DATA IMPUTATION

Data imputation is the process of replacing missing or incomplete data points in a dataset with estimated or substituted values. These estimated values are typically derived from the available data, statistical methods, or machine learning algorithms.

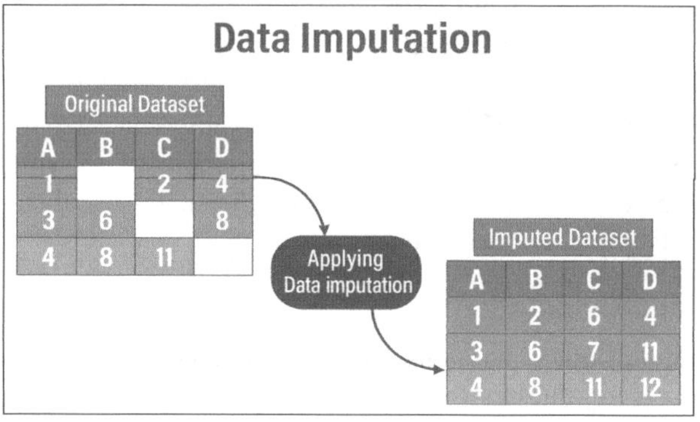

Figure 3.1: *Concept of Data Imputation*

Data imputation fills missing values in datasets, preserving data completeness and quality. It ensures practical analysis, model performance, and visualizations by preventing data loss and maintaining sample size. Imputation reduces bias, maintains data relationships, and facilitates various **statistical techniques**, enabling better decision-making and insights from incomplete data.

Importance of Data Imputation Analysis

Data imputation is crucial in data analysis as it addresses missing or incomplete data, ensuring the integrity of analyses. Imputed data enables the use of various statistical methods and machine **learning algorithms**, improving model accuracy and predictive power. Without imputation, valuable information may be lost, leading to biased or less reliable results. It helps maintain sample size, reduces bias, and enhances the overall quality and reliability of data-driven insights.

Types of Missing Data

Missing Completely at Random (MCAR)

In this type, the probability of data being missing is unrelated to both observed and unobserved data. In other words, missing is purely random and occurs by chance. MCAR implies that the missing data is not systematically related to any variables in the dataset. For example, a sensor failure that results in sporadic missing temperature readings can be considered MCAR.

Missing at Random (MAR)

Missing data is considered MAR when the probability of data being missing is related to observed data but not directly to unobserved data. In other words, missingness is dependent on some observed variables. For instance, in a medical study, men might be less likely to report certain health conditions than women, creating missing data related to the gender variable. MAR is a more general and common type of missing data than MCAR.

Missing Not at Random (MNAR)

MNAR occurs when the probability of data being missing is related to unobserved data or the missing values themselves. This type of missing data can introduce bias into analyses because the missingness is related to the missing values. An example of MNAR could be patients with severe symptoms avoiding follow-up appointments, resulting in missing data related to the severity of their condition.

Data Imputation Techniques

There are several methods and techniques for data imputation, each with its strengths and suitability depending on the nature of the data and the analysis goals. Let's discuss some commonly used data imputation techniques:

Mean/Median/Mode Imputation

- **Mean Imputation:** Replace missing values in numerical variables with the average of the observed values for that variable.
- **Median Imputation:** Replace missing values in numerical variables with the middle value of the observed values for that variable.
- **Mode Imputation:** Replace missing values in categorical variables with the most frequent category among the observed values for that variable.

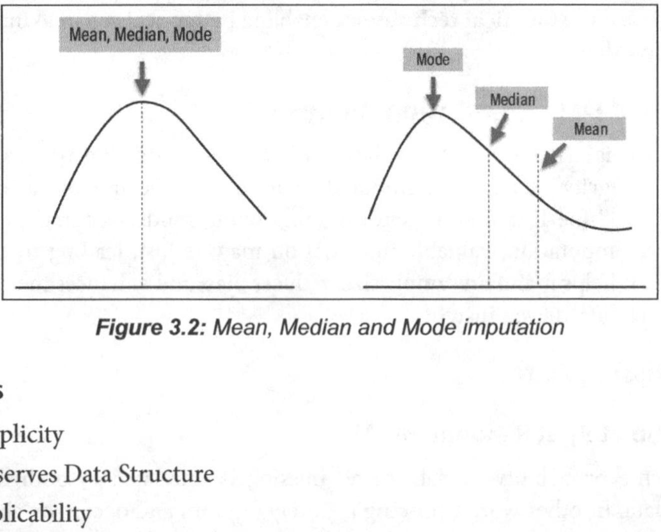

***Figure 3.2:** Mean, Median and Mode imputation*

Advantages

- Simplicity
- Preserves Data Structure
- Applicability

Disadvantages and Considerations

- Ignores Data Relationships
- May Distort Data
- Inappropriate for Missing Data Patterns

Forward Fill and Backward Fill

- **Forward Fill:** In forward fill imputation, missing values are replaced with the most recent observed value in the sequence. It propagates the last known value forward until a new observation is encountered.

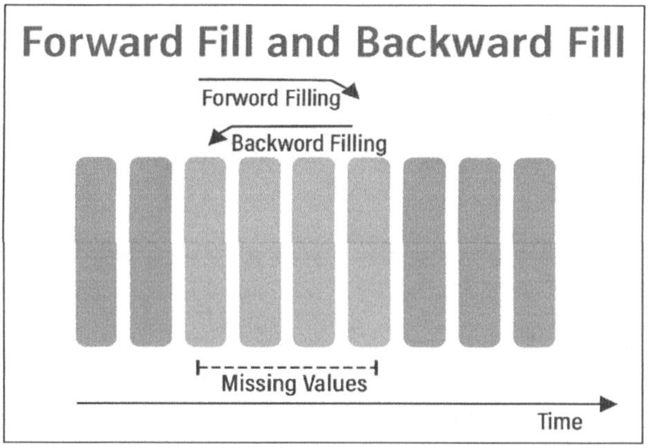

Figure 3.3: *Forward fill and Backward fill imputation*

- **Backward Fill:** In backward fill imputation, missing values are replaced with the next observed value in the sequence. It propagates the next known value backward until a new observation is encountered.

For forward fill, replace each missing value with the most recent observed value that precedes it in time. For backward fill, replace each missing value with the next observed value that follows it in time.

Advantages

- Temporal Context
- Simplicity
- Applicability

Disadvantages and Considerations

- Assumption of temporal continuity
- Potential Bias
- Missing Data Patterns

Linear Regression Imputation

Linear regression imputation is a statistical imputation technique that leverages linear regression models to predict missing values based on the relationships observed between the variable with missing data and other relevant variables in the dataset.

Steps

1. **Identify Variables:** Determine the variable with missing values (the dependent variable) and the predictor variables (independent variables) that will be used to predict the missing values.
2. **Split the Data:** Split the dataset into two subsets: one with complete data for the dependent and predictor variables and another with missing values for the dependent variable.
3. **Build a Linear Regression Model:** Use the subset with complete data to build a **linear regression model.**
4. **Predict Missing Values:** Apply the trained linear regression model to the subset with missing values to predict and fill in the missing values for the dependent variable.
5. **Evaluate Imputed Values:** Assess the quality of the imputed values by examining their distribution, checking for outliers, and comparing them to observed values where available.

Advantages

- Utilizes Relationships
- Predictive Accuracy
- Preserves Data Structure

Disadvantages and Considerations

- Assumption of Linearity
- Sensitivity to Outliers
- Model Selection

Interpolation and Extrapolation

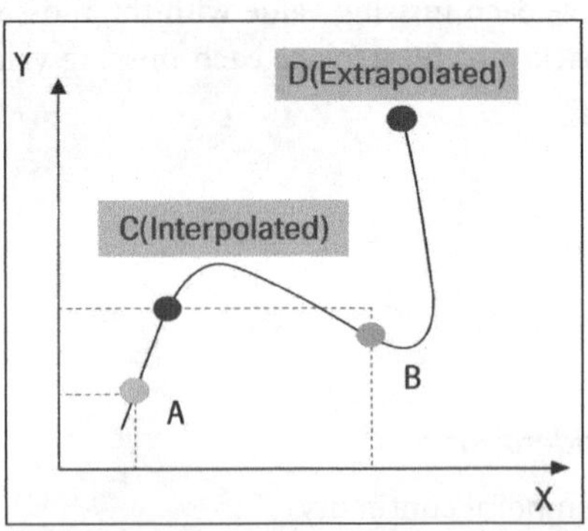

Figure 3.4: *Interpolation data imputation*

Interpolation

Interpolation is the process of estimating values between two or more known points.

Advantages

- Provide reasonable estimates within the range of observed data.
- Useful for filling gaps in data or estimating missing values.

Disadvantages and Considerations

- Assumes a continuous relationship between data points, which may not always hold.
- Accuracy decreases as you move further from the known data points.

Extrapolation

Extrapolation is the process of estimating values beyond the range of known data points.

Advantages

- Allows for making predictions or projections in the future or past.
- Useful for forecasting and trend analysis.

Disadvantages and Considerations

- Extrapolation assumes that the data trend continues, which may not always be accurate.
- Extrapolation can lead to significant errors if the underlying data pattern changes.

K-Nearest Neighbors (KNN) Imputation

K-nearest neighbors (KNN) Imputation is a method for handling missing data by estimating missing values using the values of their K-nearest neighbors, which are determined based on a similarity metric (e.g., Euclidean distance or cosine similarity) in the feature space.

Steps in KNN Imputation

- **Data Preprocessing:** Prepare the dataset by identifying the variable(s) with missing values and selecting relevant features for similarity measurement.
- **Normalization or Standardization:** Normalize or standardize the dataset to ensure that variables are on the same scale, assistance-based methods like KNN are sensitive to scale differences.
- **Distance Computation:** Calculate the distance (similarity) between data points, typically using a distance metric such as Euclidean distance, Manhattan distance, or cosine similarity.
- **Nearest Neighbors Selection:** Identify the K-nearest neighbors for each data point with missing values based on the computed distances.
- **Imputation:** Calculate the imputed value for each missing data point as a weighted average (for continuous data) or a majority vote (for categorical data) of the values from its K-nearest neighbors.
- **Repeat for All Missing Values:** Repeat the above steps for all data points with missing values, imputing each missing value separately.

Advantages

- Utilizes information from similar data points to estimate missing values
- Can capture complex relationships in the data when K is appropriately chosen.

Disadvantages and Considerations

- Sensitive to distance metric selection and a number of neighbors.

- The effectiveness of KNN imputation depends on the assumption that similar data points have similar values, which may not hold in all cases.

Expectation-maximization (EM) Imputation

Expectation-maximization (EM) imputation is an iterative statistical method for handling missing data.

Steps

1. **Model Specification:** Define a probabilistic model that represents the relationship between observed and missing data.
2. **Initialization:** Start with an initial guess of the model parameters and imputed values for missing data. Common initializations include imputing missing values with their mean or using another imputation method.
3. **Expectation (E-step):** In this step, calculate the expected values of the missing data (conditional on the observed data) using the current model parameters.
4. **Maximization (M-step):** Update the model parameters to maximize the likelihood of the observed data, given the expected values from the E-step. This involves finding parameter estimates that make the observed data most probable.
5. **Iterate**: Repeat the E-step and M-step until convergence is achieved. Convergence is typically determined by monitoring changes in in the model parameters or log-likelihood between iterations.
6. **Imputation:** Once the EM algorithm converges, use the final model parameters to impute the missing values in the dataset.

Advantages

- Can handle missing data that is not missing completely at random (i.e., data with a missing data mechanism)
- Utilizes the underlying statistical structure in the data to make imputations, potentially leading to more accurate estimates.

Disadvantages and Considerations

- **Sensitivity to model misspecification:** If the model is not a good fit for the data, imputed values may be biased.
- **Computationally intensive:** EM imputation can be computationally expensive, especially for large datasets or complex models.

Regression Trees and Random Forests

Regression Trees and Random Forests are **machine-learning techniques** used primarily for regression tasks. They are both based on **decision tree algorithms** but differ in their complexity and ability to handle complex data.

Regression Trees

Regression trees are a type **of decision tree used** for regression **analysis**. They divide the dataset into subsets, called leaves or terminal nodes, based on the input features and assign a constant value (usually the mean or median) to each leaf.

Steps

1. Start with the entire dataset.
2. Select a feature and a split point that best divides the data based on a criterion (e.g., mean squared error).
3. Repeat the splitting process for each branch until a stopping criterion is met(e.g., maximum depth or minimum number of samples per leaf).
4. Assign a constant value to each leaf, typically the mean or median of the target variable

Advantages

- Easy to interpret and visualize
- Handles both numerical and categorical data
- Can capture non-linear relationships

Disadvantages and Considerations

- Prone to overfitting, especially when the tree is deep.
- Sensitive to small variations in the data
- Single trees may not generalize well to new data

Random Forests

Random Forests are an ensemble learning technique that consists of multiple decision trees, typically built using the bagging (bootstrap aggregating) method.

Steps

1. Randomly select subsets of the data (bootstrapping) and features (feature bagging) for each tree.
2. Build individual decision trees for each subset.
3. Combine the predictions of all trees(e.g.,by averaging for regression)to make the final prediction.

Advantages

- Reduces overfitting by combining multiple models
- Provides feature importance scores

Disadvantages and Considerations

- Can be computationally expensive for a large number of trees and features.
- The resulting mode is less interpretable compared to a single decision tree

Deep Learning-Based Imputation

Deep Learning-Based Imputation is a data imputation method that uses deep neural networks to predict and fill in missing values in a dataset.

Steps

1. **Data Preprocessing:** Prepare the dataset by identifying the variable(s) with missing values and normalizing or standardizing the data as needed.

2. **Model Selection:** Choose an appropriate deep-learning architecture for imputation. Common choices include feed-forward neural networks and recurrent **neural networks (RNNs)**.
3. **Data Split:** Split the dataset into two parts: one with complete data (used for training) and another with missing values (used for imputation).
4. **Model Training:** Train the selected deep learning model using the portion of the dataset with complete data as input and the same data as output (supervised training).
5. **Imputation:** Use the trained model to predict missing values in the dataset with missing data based on the available information.
6. **Evaluation:** Assess the quality of the imputed values by comparing them to observed values where available. Common evaluation metrics include mean squared error (MSE) or mean absolute error (MAE).

Advantages

- Ability to capture complex relationships
- Data-driven imputations
- High performance

Disadvantages and Considerations

- Computational complexity.
- Data requirements
- Interpretability

Hot Deck Imputation

Hot Deck Imputation is a non-statistical imputation method that replaces missing values with observed values from similar or matching cases (donors) within the same dataset.

Steps

1. **Identify Missing Values:** Determine which variables in your data set have missing values that need to be imputed.
2. **Define matching criteria:** Specify the criteria for identifying similar or matching cases.
3. **Select Donors:** For each record with missing data, search for matching cases(donors) within the dataset based on the defined criteria.
4. **Impute Missing Values:** Replace the missing values in the target variable with values from the selected donor(s).
5. **Repeat for All Missing Values:** Continue the process for all records with missing data until all missing values are imputed.

Advantages

- Maintains dataset structure
- Simplicity
- Can be useful for small datasets or when computational resources are limited

Disadvantages and Considerations

- Assumes similarity
- Limited to existing data
- Potential for bias

Time Series Imputation

Time Series Imputation is a method used to estimate and fill in missing values within a time series dataset. It focuses on preserving the temporal relationships and patterns present in the data while addressing the gaps caused by missing observations.

Steps

1. **Data Understanding:** Begin by understanding the time series data, its context, and the reasons for missing values.
2. **Exploratory Data Analysis:** Analyze the time series to identify any patterns, trends, and seasonality that can inform the imputation process.
3. **Choose Imputation Method:** Select an appropriate imputation method based on the nature of the data and the identified patterns.
4. **Impute Missing Values:** Apply the chosen imputation method to estimate the missing values in the time series.
5. **Evaluate Imputed Values:** Assess the quality of the imputed values by comparing them to observed values where available.
6. **Sensitivity Analysis:** Conduct sensitivity analyses to assess the impact of different imputation methods and parameters on the results.
7. **Further Analysis:** Once the missing values are imputed, proceed with the intended **time series analysis**, which could include forecasting, anomaly detection, or **trend analysis**.

Advantages

- Preserves temporal relationships
- Enables continuity
- Provides a foundation for forecasting

Disadvantages and Considerations

- Requires domain knowledge
- Sensitivity to method choice
- Limited by missing data mechanism

Manual Imputation

Manual Imputation is a process in which missing values in a dataset are replaced with estimated values by human experts. It requires domain knowledge, experience, and judgment to make informed decisions about the missing data.

Steps

1. **Identify Missing Values:** First, identify the variables in your dataset that have missing values that need to be imputed.

2. **Access Domain Knowledge:** Rely on domain knowledge and expertise related to the data and the specific variables with missing values.
3. **Determine Imputation Strategy:** Decide on an appropriate strategy for imputing the missing values.
4. **Execute Imputation:** Based on the chosen strategy, manually enter the estimated values for each missing data point in the dataset.
5. **Documentation:** Keep detailed records of the imputation process, including the rationale behind the imputed values, the expert responsible for the imputation, and any relevant notes or considerations.
6. **Quality Control:** If possible, perform quality control checks or have another expert review the imputed values to ensure consistency and accuracy.

Advantages

- Domain expertise
- Flexibility
- Transparency

Disadvantages and Considerations

- Subjectivity
- Resource-intensive
- Limited to domain expertise

Best Practices for Data Imputation

Exploratory Data Analysis (EDA)

Exploratory Data Analysis (EDA) is a crucial initial step in **data analysis**, involving the visual and statistical examination of data to uncover patterns, trends, anomalies, and relationships. It helps researchers and analysts understand the data's structure, identify potential outliers, and inform subsequent data processing, modeling, and hypothesis testing. EDA typically includes summary statistics, data visualization, and data cleaning.

Data Visualization

Data Visualization is the graphical representation of data using charts, graphs, and plots. It transforms complex datasets into understandable visuals, making patterns, trends, and insights more accessible. Data visualization aids in data exploration, analysis, and communication by conveying information in a concise and visually appealing manner. It helps users interpret data, detect outliers, and make informed decisions, making it a valuable tool in various fields, including business, science, and research.

Cross-Validation

Cross-validation is a statistical technique used to evaluate the performance and generalization of machine **learning models**. It divides the dataset into training and testing subsets multiple times, ensuring that each data point is used for both training and evaluation. Cross-validation helps assess a model's robustness, detect overfitting, and estimate its predictive accuracy on unseen data.

Sensitivity Analysis

Sensitivity Analysis is a process in which variations in the parameters or assumptions of a model are systematically tested to understand how they impact the model's results or conclusions.

It helps assess the robustness and reliability of the model by identifying which factors have the most significant influence on the outcomes. Sensitivity analysis is crucial in fields like finance, engineering, and environmental science to make informed decisions and account for uncertainty.

Potential Challenges in Data Imputation

- **Missing Data Mechanisms:** Understanding the nature of missing data is crucial.
- **Bias:** The imputation method can introduce bias if it systematically underestimates or overestimates missing values.
- **Imputation Model Selection:** Choosing the right imputation model or method can be challenging, especially when dealing with complex data.
- **High-Dimensional Data:** In datasets with a large number of features (high dimensionality), imputation becomes more complex.

Future Developments in Data Imputation Techniques

Future developments in data imputation will likely focus on advancing machine learning-based techniques, such as deep **learning models**, to handle complex datasets with high dimensionality.

Additionally, there will be an increased emphasis on addressing missing data mechanisms like Missing Not at Random (MNAR) through innovative modeling approaches.

3.2 DATA TRANSFORMATION

In the rapidly evolving landscape of data-driven decision-making and innovation, the ability to effectively leverage information is paramount. With an increasing reliance on data analytics and data science, it is essential to recognize that raw data often requires a touch of refinement before it can be harnessed for valuable insights. Enter the world of data transformation: a vital step that ensures your dataset is well-suited for accurate analysis and model training.

Data transformation involves a range of techniques designed to make a dataset more suitable for analysis and other applications, such as training machine learning models. This can include cleaning, formatting, and deleting data as required, making the information more accessible, structured, and easy to interpret. As datasets vary in quality and structure, transforming them into a usable format is crucial for extracting value and driving better outcomes.

There are numerous methods available for effective data transformation, each catering to different project requirements and dataset characteristics. In this blogpost, we will outline the most common data transformation techniques, highlight their benefits, and help you choose the best techniques for you. By mastering these methods, you'll be well-equipped to prepare your data for insightful analysis and to build more accurate, reliable machine-learning models.

Benefits of Data Transformation

1. **Improved data quality:** Data transformation helps identify and correct inconsistencies, errors, and missing values, leading to cleaner and more accurate data for analysis.
2. **Enhanced data integration:** By converting data into a standardized format, data transformation enables data integration from multiple sources, fostering collaboration and data sharing among different systems.
3. **Better decision making and business intelligence:** With clean and integrated data, organizations can make more informed decisions based on accurate insights, which improves efficiency and competitiveness.
4. **Scalability:** Data transformation helps teams manage increasing volumes of data, allowing organizations to scale their data processing and analytics capabilities as needed.
5. **Data privacy:** Protect data privacy and comply with data protection regulations by transforming sensitive data through techniques like anonymization, pseudonymization, or encryption.
6. **Improved data visualization:** Transforming data into appropriate formats or aggregating it in meaningful ways makes it easier to create engaging and insightful data visualizations.
7. **Easier machine learning:** Data transformation prepares data for machine learning algorithms by converting it into a suitable format and addressing issues like missing values or class imbalance, which can improve model performance.
8. **Time and cost savings:** By automating data transformation processes, organizations can reduce the time and effort needed for data preparation, allowing data scientists and analysts to focus on higher-value tasks

Types of Data Transformation

- **Constructive Transformations:** Constructive transformations create new data attributes or features within the dataset, or enhance existing ones to improve the quality and effectiveness of data analysis or machine learning models. These transformations add value to the dataset by generating additional information or by providing a better representation of existing data, making it more suitable for analysis.
- **Destructive Transformations:** Destructive transformations remove unnecessary or irrelevant data from the dataset, and streamline the information to be more focused and efficient for analysis or modeling. This can include data cleaning (removing duplicates, correcting errors), dealing with missing values (imputation or deletion), and feature selection (eliminating redundant or irrelevant features). By reducing noise and distractions, destructive transformations contribute to more accurate insights and improved model performance.
- **Aesthetic Transformations:** Aesthetic transformations deal with the presentation and organization, ensuring it is easily understandable and visually appealing for human
- **Interpretation:** These transformations include data standardization (converting data to a common format), sorting, and formatting. While aesthetic transformations

may not directly affect the analytical or predictive power of the data, they play a vital role in facilitating efficient data exploration and communication of insights.

- **Structural Transformations:** Structural transformations involve modifying the overall structure and organization of the dataset, making it more suitable for analysis or machine learning models. They are useful in time series analysis, multi-source data integration, preparing data for machine learning, data warehousing, and data visualization.

Ways of Data Transformation

There are several different ways to transform data,such as:

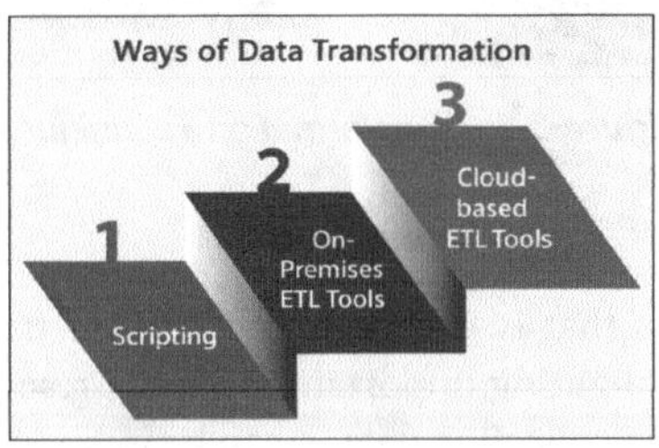

Figure 3.5: *Different ways of transformation*

- **Scripting:** Data transformation through scripting involves **Python or SQL to write** the code to extract and transform data. Python and SQL are scripting languages that allow you to automate certain tasks in a program. They also allow you to extract information from data sets. Scripting languages require less code than traditional programming languages. Therefore, it is less intensive.
- **On-Premises ETL Toolse**t tools take the required work to script the data transformation by automating the process. On-premises ETL tools are hosted on company servers. While these tools can help save you time, using them often **requires extensive expertise and significant infrastructure costs**.
- **Cloud-Based ETL Tools:** As the name suggests, cloud-based ETL tools are **hosted in the cloud**. These tools are often the easiest for non-technical users to utilize. They allow you to collect data from any cloud source and load it into your data warehouse. With cloud-based ETL tools, you can decide how often you want to pull data from your source, **and you can monitor your usage**.

There are two types of data integration processes, ETL(Extract, Transform, Load) and ELT (Extract, Load, Transform). Both of these data integration processes are commonly used in data warehousing and data management. The main difference between ETL and ELT is the order in which the transformation stage is performed. ETL involves transforming data into a suitable format in the data pipeline itself, before loading it into the data warehouse. This is especially useful for structured event data that requires significant transformation before reaching its destination.

In contrast, ELT involves loading data into data warehouses first, and performing the transformation once the data is in the warehouse, making it useful for unstructured or semi-structured data that requires less transformation and can be done more efficiently in the target system. Choosing ETL or ELT depends on the complexity and type of transformation you want to perform. Learn more about different methods and use cases for transforming data with Rudder Stack in the docs.

Data Transformation Techniques

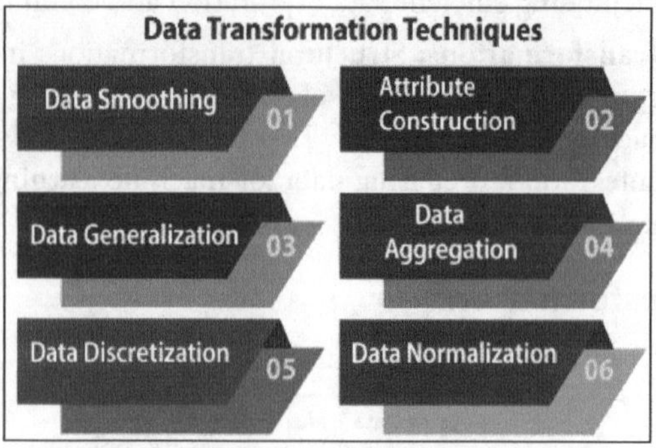

***Figure 3.6:** Transformation Techniques*

Data Smoothing

Data smoothing is a process that is used to remove noise from the dataset using some algorithms. It allows for highlighting important features present in the dataset. It helps in predicting the patterns. When collecting data, it can be manipulated to eliminate or reduce any variance or any other noise form.

The concept behind data smoothing is that it will be able to identify simple changes to help predict different trends and patterns. This serves as a help to analysts or traders who need to look at a lot of data which can often be difficult to digest for finding patterns that they wouldn't see otherwise. We have seen how the noise is removed from the data using the techniques such as binning, regression, clustering.

- **Binning:** This method splits the sorted data into the number of bins and smoothens the data values in each bin considering the neighborhood values around it.
- **Regression:** This method identifies the relation among two dependent attributes so that if we have one attribute, it can be used to predict the other attribute.
- **Clustering:** This method groups similar data values and form a cluster. The values that lie outside a cluster are known as outliers.

Attribute Construction

In the attribute construction method, the new attributes consult the existing attributes to construct a new data set that eases data mining. New attributes are created and applied to assist the mining process from the given attributes. This simplifies the original data and makes the mining more efficient. For example, suppose we have a data set referring to measurements of different plots, i.e., we may have the height and width of each plot. So here, we can construct a new attribute 'area' from attributes 'height' and 'weight'. This also helps understand the relations among the attributes in a data set.

Data Aggregation

Data collection or aggregation is the method of storing and presenting data in a summary format. The data may be obtained from multiple data sources to integrate these data sources into a data analysis description. This is a crucial step since the accuracy of data analysis insights is highly dependent on the quantity and quality of the data used.

Gathering accurate data of high quality and a large enough quantity is necessary to produce relevant results. The collection of data is useful for everything from decisions concerning financing or business strategy of the product, pricing, operations, and marketing strategies. For example, we have a data set of sales reports of an enterprise that has quarterly sales of each year. We can aggregate the data to get the enterprise's annual sales report.

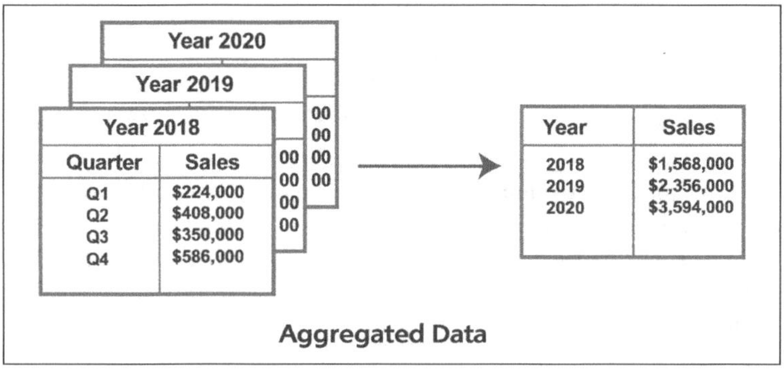

***Figure 3.7:** Data Aggregation*

Data Normalization

Normalizing the data refers to scaling the data values to a much smaller range such as [-1, 1] or [0.0, 1.0]. There are different methods to normalize the data, as discussed below. Consider that we have a numeric attribute A and we have n number of observed values for attribute A that are V1, V2, V3, ...Vn.

- **Min-max normalization:** This method implements a linear transformation on the original data. Let us consider that we have minAand maxAas the minimum and maximum value observed for attribute A and Vi is the value for attribute A that has to be normalized. The min-max normalization would map Vi to the V'i in a new smaller range [new_minA, new_maxA]. The formula for min-max normalization is given below:

$$V'_i = \frac{vi - min_A}{max_A - min_A}(newmaxA - newmin_A) + new\_min_A$$

$$\frac{73600-1200}{9800-1200}(1.0 - 0.0) + 0.0 = 0.716$$

For example, we have $1200 and $9800 as the minimum, and maximum value for the attribute income, and [0.0,1.0]is the range in which we have to map a value of $73,600. The value $73,600 would be transformed using min-max normalization as follows:

- **Z-score normalization:** This method normalizes the value for attribute A using the **mean**a nd **standard deviation**. The following formula is used for Z-score normalization:

$$v'_i = \frac{vi - `}{^A}$$

Here Ā and σA are the mean and standard deviation for attribute A, respectively. For example, we have a mean and standard deviation for attribute A as $54,000 and $16,000. And we have to normalize the value $73,600 using z-score normalization.

$$\frac{73600-5400}{1600}=1.225$$

- **Decimal Scaling:** This method normalizes the value of attribute A by moving the decimal point in the value. This movement of a decimal point depends on the maximum absolute value of A. The formula for the decimal scaling is given below:

$$v'_i = \frac{v_i}{10^j}$$

Here j is the smallest integer such that $\max(|v'i|)<1$ For example, the observed values for attribute A range from -986 to 917, and the maximum absolute value for attribute A is 986. Here, to normalize each value of attribute A using decimal scaling, we have to divide each value of attributeAby1000, i.e., j=3.So, the value -986 would be normalized to -0.986, and 917 would be normalized to 0.917. The normalization parameters such as mean, standard deviation, the maximum absolute value must be preserved to normalize the future data uniformly.

Data Discretization

This is a process of converting continuous data into a set of data intervals. Continuous attribute values are substituted by small interval labels. This makes the data easier to study and analyze. If a data mining task handles a continuous attribute, then its discrete values can be replaced by constant quality attributes. This improves the efficiency of the task.

This method is also called a data reduction mechanism as it transforms a large dataset into a set of categorical data. Discretization also uses decision tree-based algorithms to produce short, compact, and accurate results when using discrete values.

Data discretization can be classified into two types: **supervised discretization**, where the class information is used, and **unsupervised discretization**, which is based on which direction the process proceeds, i.e., 'top-down splitting strategy' or 'bottom-up merging strategy'.

For example, the values for the age attribute can be replaced by the interval labels such as (0- 10, 11-20…) or (kid, youth, adult, senior).

Data Generalization

It converts low-level data attributes to high-level data attributes using concept hierarchy. This conversion from a lower level to a higher conceptual level is useful to get a clearer picture of the data. Data generalization can be divided into two approaches:

- Data cube process (OLAP) approach.
- Attribute-oriented induction (AOI)approach.

Data Transformation Process

The entire process for transforming data is known as **ETL(Extract, Load, and Transform)**. Through the ETL process, analysts can convert data to its desired format.

Here are the steps involved in the data transformation process:

1. **Data Discovery**: During the first stage, analysts work to understand and identify data in its source format. To do this, they will use data profiling tools. This step helps analysts decide what they need to do to get data into its desired format.

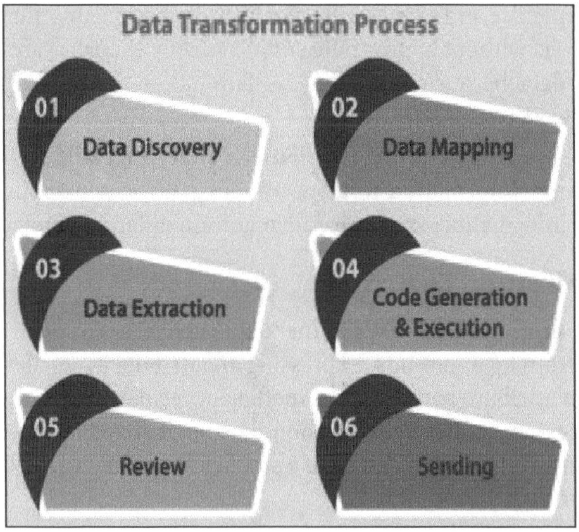

Figure 3.8: *Process of Data Transformation*

2. **Data Mapping:** During this phase, analysts perform data mapping to determine how individual fields are modified, mapped, filtered, joined, and aggregated. Data mapping is essential to many data processes, and one misstep can lead to incorrect analysis and ripple through your entire organization.
3. **Data Extraction:** During this phase, analysts extract the data from its original source. These may include structured sources such as databases or streaming sources such as customer log files from web applications.
4. **Code Generation and Execution:** Once the data has been extracted, analysts need to create a code to complete the transformation. Often, analysts generate codes with the help of data transformation platforms or tools.
5. **Review:** After transforming the data, analysts need to check it to ensure everything has been formatted correctly.
6. **Sending:** The final step involves sending the data to its target destination. The target might be a data warehouse or a database that handles both structured and unstructured data.

Disadvantages of Data Transformation

While data transformation comes with a lot of benefits, still there are some challenges to transforming data effectively, such as:

- Data transformation can be **expensive**. The cost is dependent on the specific infrastructure, software, and tools used to process data. Expenses may include licensing, computing resources, and hiring necessary personnel.
- Data transformation processes can be **resource-intensive**. Performing transformations in an on-premises data warehouse after loading or transforming data before feeding it into applications can create a computational burden that slows down other operations. If you use a cloud-based data warehouse, you can do the transformations after loading because the platform can scale up to meet demand.

- **Lack of expertise** and carelessness can introduce problems during transformation. Data analysts without appropriate subject matter expertise are less likely to notice incorrect data because they are less familiar with the range of accurate and permissible values.
- Enterprises can perform **transformations that don't suit** their needs. A business might change information to a specific format for one application only to then revert the information to its prior format for a different application.

Minmax Normalization Overview

The measurement unit used can affect the data analysis. For instance, changing the measurement unit from kg to pounds. Expressing an attribute in smaller units will lead to a larger range for that attribute and thus give inefficient results. To avoid the dependence on the choice of measurement units, the data should be normalized. Normalization is used for scaling the data of attributes so that it falls in a smaller range, such as -2.0 to 2.0. It is usually used in classification algorithms.

Use of Normalization

Normalization is required when we deal with attributes having a different scale, and it may lead to less effectiveness of an important attribute (having a lower scale) because of other attributes having values on a larger scale. It also decreases the training time needed for the machine to learn the data. Thus, the efficiency of the machine learning model increases after the dataset is normalized.

Min-Max Normalization

In this technique of knowledge normalization, a linear transformation is performed on the first data. Minimum and maximum value from data is fetched and each value is replaced according to the following formula. Min-Max Normalization preserves the relationships among the original data values. It will encounter an out-of-bounds error if a future input case for normalization falls outside the first data range for A.

The formula is given below:

$$V' = V - min(A)|max(A) - min(A)(new_{m}ax(A) - new_{m}in(A)) + new_{m}in(A)$$

Where A is the attribute data represent as follows.

```
in(A)- It is the minimum absolute value A.
Max(A)- It is maximum absolute value of A.v' - It is the new value of each attribute data. v      - It is the old value of each attribute data.
new_max(A), new_min(A) is the max and min value within the range (i.e boundary value of range required) respectively.
Min-Max Normalization maps a value v of A to v'in the range [new_min(A),new_max(A)] by computing.
```

Example

Normalize the following group of data

```
1000,2000,3000,9000
using min-maxnormalizationbysettingmin:0andmax:1
```

Solution

```
here, new_max(A)=1 , as given in question-
max=1 new_min(A)=0,as given in question-
min=0
max(A)=9000,as the maximum data among 1000,2000,3000,9000 is 9000
min(A)=1000,as the minimum data among 1000,2000,3000,9000 is 1000
```

Case-1: Normalizing1000

```
 v=1000 , putting all values in the formula, we
 get v'=(1000-1000) X (1-0)
                     +0=0
------------
9000-1000
```

Case-2: Normalizing2000

```
 v=2000 , putting all values sin the formula, we get
 v'=(2000-1000) X (1-0)
                     +0=0.125
------------
9000-1000
```

Case-3: Normalizing3000

```
 v=3000 , putting all values sin the formula, we get
 v'=(3000-1000) X (1-0)
                     +0=0.25
------------
9000-1000
```

Case-4: Normalizing9000

```
v=9000 , putting all values sin the formula, we
get v'=(9000-1000) X (1-0)
                     +0=1
------------
9000-1000
```

Outcome:

Hence, the normalized values of 1000,2000,3000,9000are0,0.125,.25,1.

z-Transform

A z-score describes the position of a raw score in terms of its distance from the mean when measured in standard deviation units. The z-score is positive if the value lies above the mean and negative if it lies below the mean. It is also known as a standard score because it allows the comparison of scores on different kinds of variables by standardizing the distribution. A standard normal distribution (SND) isa normally shaped distribution with a mean of 0 and a standard deviation (SD) of 1

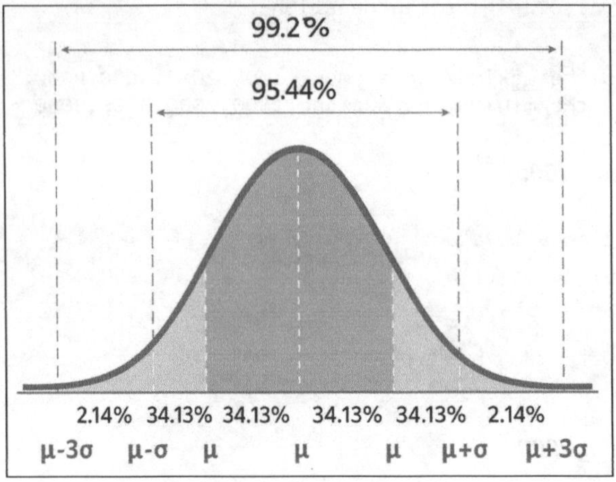

***Figure 3.9:** Z-Score transformation*

Characteristics of Z-Score

- The magnitude of the Z-score reflects how far a data point is from the mean in terms of standard deviations.
- An element having a z-scoreoflessthan0representsthattheelementislessthanthe mean.
- Z-scores allow for the comparison of data points from different distributions.
- An element having a z-scoregreaterthan0representsthattheelementisgreaterthan the mean.
- An element having a z-scoreequalto0representsthattheelementisequaltothemean.
- An element having a z-scoreequalto1represents that the element is 1 standard deviation greater than the mean; a z-score equal to 2, 2 standard deviations greater than the mean, and so on.
- An element having a z-score equal to -1 represents that the element is 1 standard deviation less than the mean; a z-score equal to -2, 2 standard deviations less than the mean, and so on.
- If the number of elements in a given set is large, then about 68% of the elements have az-score between -1 and 1; about 95% have a z-score between-2 and 2; about99%have a z-score between -3 and 3. This is known as the Empirical Rule, and it states the percentage of data within certain standard deviations from the mean in a normal distribution.

Sometimes one has the problem to make two samples comparable, i.e. to compare measured values of a sample with respect to their (relative) position in the distribution. An often-used aid is the **z-transform** which converts the values of a sample into z-scores:

$$Z_j = \frac{X_i - \bar{X}}{S}$$

z_i...z-transformed sample observations x_i... original values of the sample

$\overline{X}$... sample mean X

s... standard deviation of the sample

The z-transform is also called **standardization** or **auto-scaling**. z-scores become comparable by measuring the observations in multiples of the standard deviation of that sample. The mean of a z-transformed sample is always zero. If the original distribution is a normal one, the z-transformed data belong to a standard normal distribution (μ=0, s=1).

The following example demonstrates the effect of the standardization of the data. Assume we have two normal distributions, one with mean of 10.0 and a standard deviation of 30.0 (top left), the other with a mean of 200 and a standard deviation of 20.0 (top right). The standardization of both data sets results in comparable distributions since both z-transformed distributions have a mean of 0.0 and a standard deviation of 1.0 (bottom row).

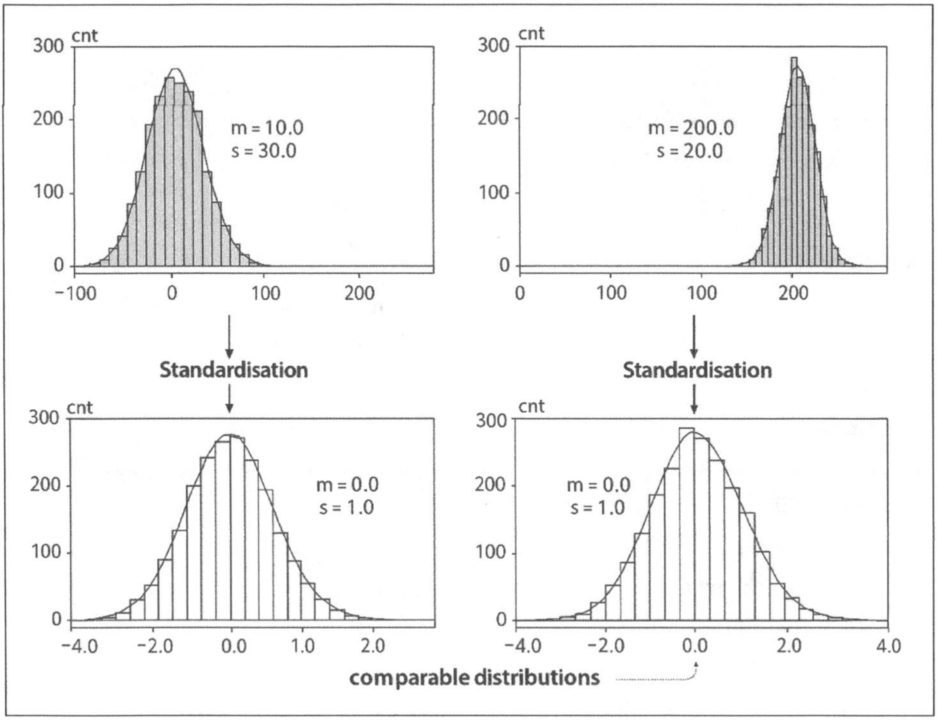

Figure 3.10: *Data Standardization*

Problems

1. Scores on a psychological well-being scale range from 1 to 10, with an average score of 6 and a standard deviation of 2. What is the z-score for a person who scored 4?
2. On a measure of anxiety, a group of participants show a mean score of 35 with a standard deviation of 5. What is the z-score corresponding to a score of 30?
3. A depression inventory has an average score of 50 with a standard deviation of10. What is the z-score corresponding to a score of 70?

4. In a study on sleep, participants report an average of 7 hours of sleeper night, with a standard deviation of 1 hour. What is the z-score for a person reporting 5 hours of sleep?
5. On a memory test, the average score is 100, with a standard deviation of 15. What is the z- score corresponding to a score of 85?
6. A happiness scale has an average score of 75 with a standard deviation of 10. What is the z-score corresponding to a score of 95?
7. An intelligence test has a mean score of 100 with a standard deviation of 15. What is the z- score that corresponds to a score of 130?

Answers for Sample Questions

1. Z-score=(4–6)/2 =-1
2. Z-score=(30–35)/5=-1
3. Z-score=(70– 50)/10 =2
4. Z-score=(5–7)/1 =-2
5. Z-score=(85–100)/15 =-1
6. Z-score=(95– 75)/10 =2
7. Z-score=(130– 100)/15 =2

Example

You take the GATE examination and score 500. The mean score for the GATE is 390 and the standard deviation is 45. How well did you score on the test compared to the average test taker?

Solution

Following data is readily available in the above question statement Raw score/observed value = X = 500

Mean score = μ = 390 Standard deviation = σ = 45

By applying the formula of z-score, $z = (X - \mu) / \sigma$

z=(500–390)/45

z=110/45=2.44 z-score is **2.44.**

Since the Z-Score is positive 2.44, we will make use of the positive Z-Table.

Now let's take a look at Z Table (CC-BY) to know how well you scored compared to the other test-takers.

Follow the instructions below to find the probability from the table.

Here, **z-score=2.44,** which indicates that the data point is 2.44 standard deviations above the mean.

1. Firstly, map the first two digits2.4ontheY-axis.
2. Then along the X-axis, map0.04
3. Join both axes. The intersection of the two will provide you the cumulative probability associated with the Z-score value you're looking for

Table 3.1: *Normal distribution table*

Z	0	0.01	0.02	0.03	0.04	0.05	0.06	0.07
1.7	0.95543	0.95637	0.95728	0.95818	0.95907	0.95994	0.9608	0.96164
1.8	0.96407	0.96485	0.96562	0.96638	0.96712	0.96784	0.96856	0.96926
1.9	0.97128	0.97193	0.97257	0.9732	0.97381	0.97441	0.975	0.97558
2	0.97725	0.97778	0.97831	0.97882	0.97932	0.97982	0.9803	0.98077
2.1	0.98214	0.98257	0.983	0.98341	0.98382	0.98422	0.98461	0.985
2.2	0.9861	0.98645	0.98679	0.98713	0.98745	0.98778	0.98809	0.9884
2.3	0.98928	0.98956	0.98983	0.9901	0.99036	0.99061	0.99086	0.99111
2.4	0.9918	0.99202	0.99224	0.99245	0.99266	0.99286	0.99305	0.99324
2.5	0.99379	0.99396	0.99413	0.9943	0.99446	0.99461	0.99477	0.99492
2.6	0.99534	0.99547	0.9956	0.99573	0.99585	0.99598	0.99609	0.99621
2.7	0.99653	0.99664	0.99674	0.99683	0.99693	0.99702	0.99711	0.9972

As a result, you will get the final value which is **0.99266.**

Now, we need to compare how our original score of 500 on the GATE examination compares to the average score of the batch. To do that we need to convert the cumulative probability associated with the Z-score into a percentage value of 0.99266×100=99.266% Finally, you can say that you have performed well than almost 99% of other test-takers.

Log Transform

The Log Transform is one of the most popular Transformation techniques out there. It is primarily used to convert as skewed distribution to a normal distribution/less-skewed distribution. In this transform, we take the log of the values in a column and use these values as the column instead.

When our original continuous data do not follow the bell curve, we can log transform this data to make it as "normal" as possibles of that the statistical analysis results from this data become more valid. In other words, the log transformation reduces or removes the skewness of our original data. The important caveat there is that the original dataset follows or approximately follows a log-normal distribution. Otherwise, the log transformation won't work.

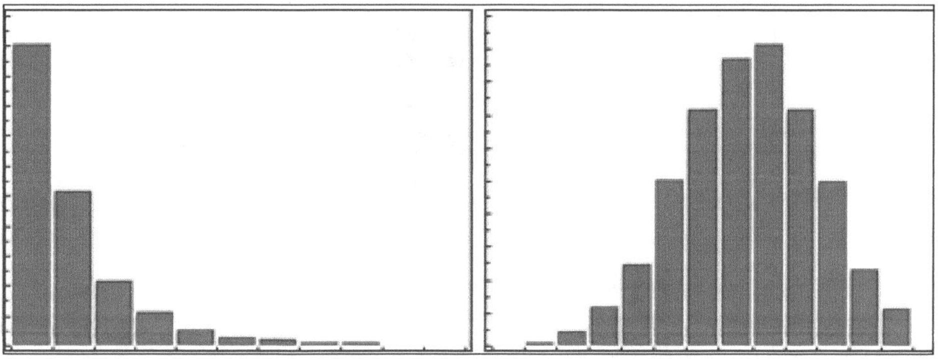

Figure 3.11: *Log-normal distribution*

It is because the log function is equipped to deal with large numbers. Here is an example: log(10) = 1 log(100) = 2, and log(10000) = 4.

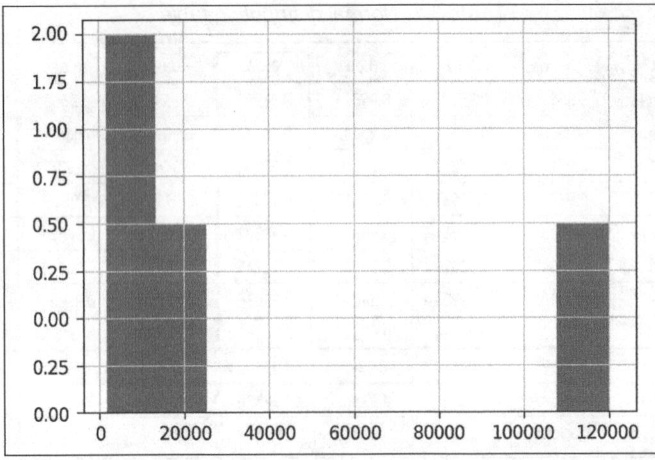

Figure 3.12: *Histogram*

Thus, in our example, while plotting the histogram of Income, it ranges from 0 to 1,20,000:

Let us see what happens when we apply log on this column: df['log_income'] = np.log(df['Income'])

- Reducing the impact of too-low values
- Reducing the impact of too-high values.

	Income	Age	Department	log_income
0	15000	25	HR	9.615805
1	1800	18	Legal	7.495542
2	120000	42	Marketing	11.695247
3	10000	51	Management	9.210340

Figure 3.13: *Sample Data frame*

A small cave at though – if our data has negative values or values ranging from 0 to 1, we cannot apply log transform directly– since the log of negative numbers and numbers between 0 and 1 is undefined, we would get error or NaN values in our data. In such cases, we can add a number to these values to make them all greater than 1. Then, we can apply the log transform.

Let us plot a histogram of the above, using 5 bins: df['log_income'].plot.hist(bins = 5)

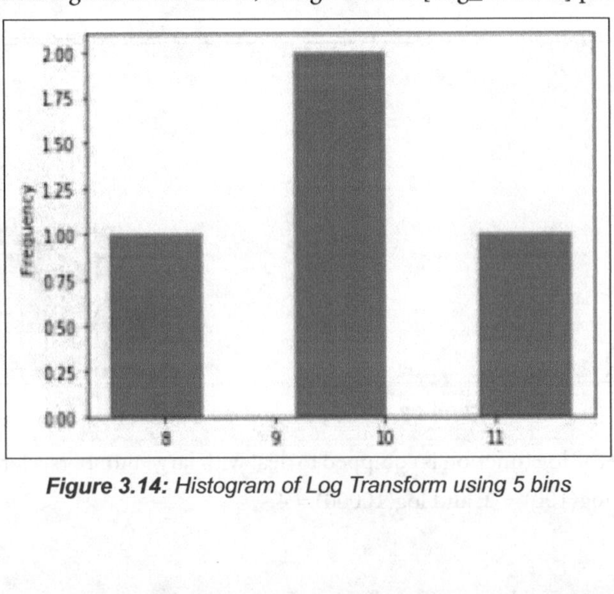

Figure 3.14: *Histogram of Log Transform using 5 bins*

3.3 BINNING, CLASSING AND TRANSFORMATION

Data binning, also called discrete binning or bucketing, is a data pre-processing technique used to reduce the effects of minor observation errors. It is a form of quantization. The original data values are divided into small intervals known as bins, and then they are replaced by a general value calculated for that bin. This has a smoothing effect on the input data and may also reduce the chances of over fitting in the case of small datasets.

Statistical data binning is a way to group numbers of more or less continuous values into a smaller number of "bins". It can also be used in multivariate statistics, binning in several dimensions simultaneously. For example, if you have data about a group of people, you might want to arrange their ages into a smaller number of age intervals, such as grouping every five years together.

Binning can dramatically improve resource utilization and model build response time without significant loss in model quality. Binning can improve model quality by strengthening the relationship between attributes.

Supervised binning is a form of intelligent binning in which important characteristics of the data are used to determine the bin boundaries. In supervised binning, the bin boundaries are identified by a single-predictor decision tree that considers the joint distribution with the target. Supervised binning can be used for both numerical and categorical attributes.

Image Data Processing

In the context of image processing, binning is the procedure of combining a cluster of pixels into a single pixel. As such, in 2x2 binning, an array of 4 pixels becomes a single larger pixel, reducing the overall number of pixels.

Although associated with loss of information, this aggregation reduces the amount of data to be processed, facilitating the analysis. For example, binning the data may also reduce the impact of reading noise on the processed image (at the cost of a lower resolution).

Why is Binning Used?

Binning or discretization is used to transform a continuous or numerical variable into a categorical feature. Binning of continuous variables introduces non-linearity and tends to improve the performance of the model. It can also be used to identify missing values or outliers.

Example of Binning

Histograms are an example of data binning used to observe underlying distributions. They typically occur in one-dimensional space and equal intervals for ease of visualization.

Binning is also used in machine learning to speed up the decision-tree boosting method for supervised classification and regression in algorithms such as Microsoft's Light GBM and scikit-learn's Histogram-based Gradient Boosting Classification Tree.

How do you Binning Data?

There are two methods of dividing data into bins and binning data:

1. **Equal Frequency Binning:** Bins have an equal frequency.

   For example, equal frequency:

Input: [5, 10, 11, 13, 15, 35, 50, 55, 72, 92, 204, 215]

Output

[5,10, 11, 13]

[15,35, 50, 55]

[72,92, 204, 215]

2. Equal Width Binning: Bins have equal width with a range of each bin are defined as [min +w],[min+2w]....[min+nw]where w=(max -min)/(no of bins). For example, equal Width:

   Input:[5, 10, 11, 13, 15, 35, 50, 55, 72, 92, 204, 215]

   Output

   [5,10, 11, 13, 15, 35, 50, 55, 72]

   [92]

   [204,215]

3.4 DATA STANDARDIZATION

Data standardization comes into the picture when features of the input data set have large differences between their ranges, or simply when measured in different units (e.g., pounds, meters, miles, etc.). These differences in the ranges of initial features cause trouble for many machine learning models. For example, for the models that are based on distance computation, if one of the features has a broad range of values, the distance will be governed by this particular feature.

Definition

Data standardization is an important technique that mostly performs the data pre-processing step before imputing data into many machine learning models to standardize the range of features of an input data set.

To illustrate this with an example: Say we have a two-dimensional dataset with two features, height in meters and weight in pounds, that range respectively from 1 to 2 meters and 10 to 200 pounds. No matter what distance-based model you perform on this data set, the weight feature will dominate over the height feature and will have more contribution to the distance computation, just because it has bigger values compared to the height. So, to prevent this problem, transforming features to comparable scales using standardization is the solution.

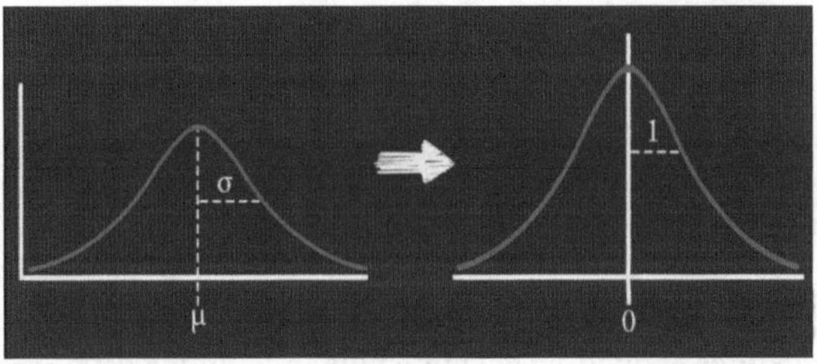

Figure 3.15: Sample data standardization

How to Standardize Data

Z-Score

Z-score is one of the most popular methods to standardize data, and can be done by subtracting the mean and dividing by the standard deviation for each value of each feature.

$$z = \frac{value - mean}{standard\ \ deviation}$$

Once the standardization is done, all the features will have a mean of zero and a standard deviation of one, and thus, the same scale.

When and Why to Standardize Data

As seen above, for distance-based models, standardization is performed to prevent features with wider ranges from dominating the distance metric. But the reason we standardize data is not the same for all machine learning models and differs from one model to another.

1. Before Principal Component Analysis (PCA)

In principal component analysis, features with high variances or wide ranges get more weight than those with low variances, and consequently, they end up illegitimately dominating the first principal components (components with maximum variance). I used the word "illegitimately" here because the reason these features have high variances compared to the other ones is just because they were measured in different scales.

2. Before Clustering

Clustering models are distance-based algorithms. In order to measure similarities between observations and form clusters they use a distance metric. So, features with high ranges will have a bigger influence on the clustering. Therefore, standardization is required before building a clustering model.

3. Before K-Nearest Neighbors (KNN)

K-nearest neighbors is a distance-based classifier that classifies new observations based on similar measures (e.g., distance metrics) with labeled observations of the training set.

Standardization makes all variables contribute equally to the similarity measures.

4. Before Support Vector Machine (SVM)

The support vector machine tries to maximize the distance between the separating plane and the support vectors. If one feature has very large values, it will dominate over other features when calculating the distance. Standardization gives all features the same influence on the distance metric.

5. Before Measuring Variable Importance in Regression Models

You can measure variable importance in regression analysis by fitting a regression model using the standardized independent variables and comparing the absolute value of their standardized coefficients. But, if the independent variables are not standardized, comparing their coefficients becomes meaningless.

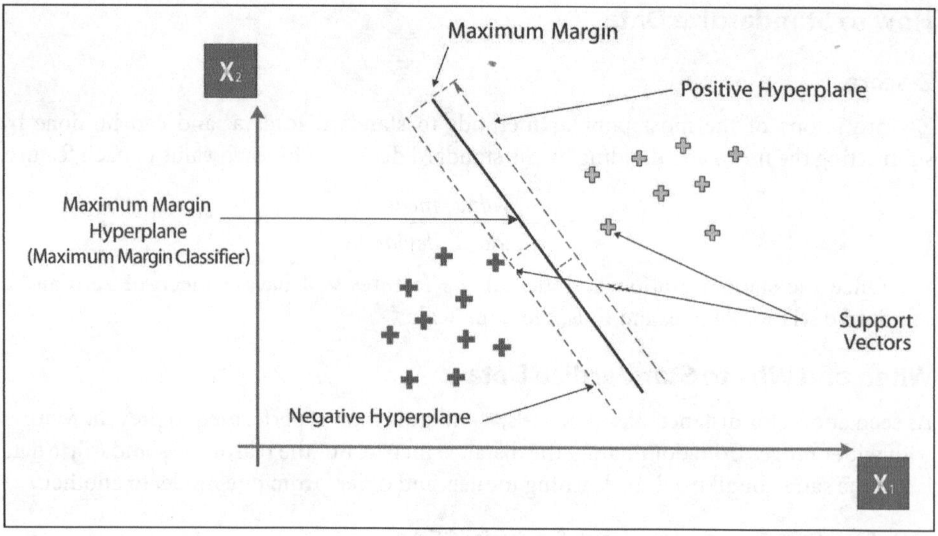

Figure 3.16

6. Before Lasso And Ridge Regressions

Lasso and ridge regressions place a penalty on the magnitude of the coefficients associated with each variable, and the scale of variables will affect how much of a penalty will be applied to their coefficients. The coefficients of variables with a large variance are small and thus less penalized. Therefore, standardization is required before fitting both regressions.

Logistic Regressions and Tree-Based Models

Logistic regressions and tree-based algorithms such as decision trees, random forests, and gradient boosting are not sensitive to the magnitude of variables. So standardization is not needed before fitting these kinds of models.

Benefits of Data Standardization

Data standardization transforms data into a consistent, standard format, making it easier to understand and use—especially for machine learning models and across different computer systems and databases.

Standardized data can facilitate data processing and storage tasks, as well as improve accuracy during data analysis. Plus, making data more navigable by standardizing it can reduce costs and save time for businesses.

Normalization vs. Data Standardization

Normalization involves scaling data values in a range between zero and one ([0,1]) or between negative one and one ([-1, 1]). Data standardization, on the other hand, involves scaling data values so that they have a mean of zero and a standard deviation of one. Also, since normalization has a restricted range and standardization does not, normalization is more likely to be affected by outliers, whereas standardization is less likely to be affected by outliers. Normalization is useful for when a distribution is unknown or not normal (not bell curve), while standardization is useful for normal distributions.

3.5 OUTLIERS

What is an Outlier?

An outlier is a data point that significantly deviates from the rest of the data. It can be either much higher or much lower than the other data points, and its presence can have a significant impact on the results of machine learning algorithms. They can be caused by measurement or execution errors. The analysis of outlier data is referred to as outlier analysis or outlier mining.

Algorithm

1. Calculate the mean of each cluster
2. Initialize the Threshold value
3. Calculate the distance of the test data from each cluster mean
4. Find the nearest cluster to the test data
5. *(Distance>Threshold) then, Outlier*

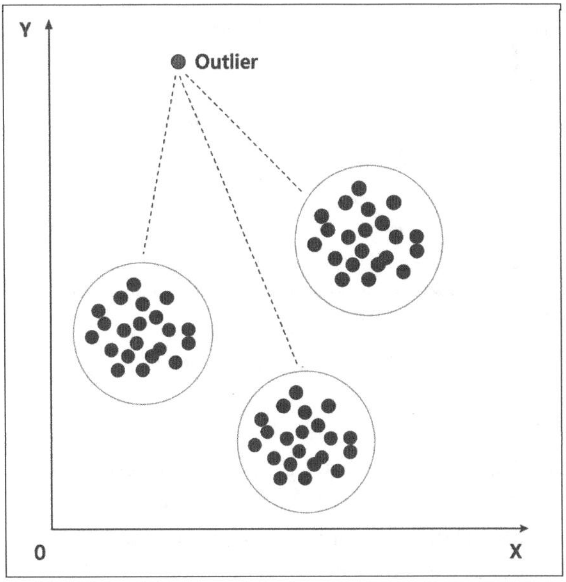

Figure 3.17: *Outliers*

Types of Outliers

Outliers are of three types, namely:

1. Global (or Point) Outliers
2. Collective Outliers
3. Contextual (or Conditional) Outliers

1. Global Outliers

1. **Definition:** Global outliers are data points that deviate significantly from the overall distribution of a dataset.

2. **Causes:** Errors in data collection, measurement errors, or truly unusual events can result in global outliers.
3. **Impact:** Global outliers can distort data analysis results and affect machine learning model performance.
4. **Detection:** Techniques include statistical methods (e.g., z-score, Mahalanob is distance), machine learning algorithms (e.g., isolation forest, one-class SVM), and data visualization techniques.
5. **Handling:** Options may include removing or correcting outliers, transforming data, or using robust methods.
6. **Considerations:** Carefully considering the impact of global outliers is crucial for accurate data analysis and machine learning model outcomes.

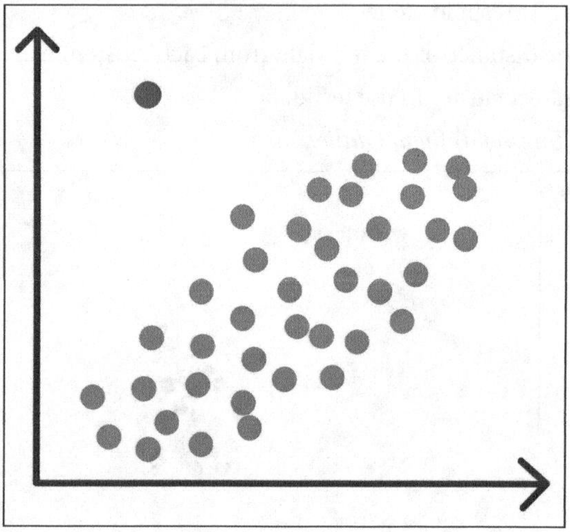

Figure 3.18: Global Outlier

2. Collective Outliers

1. **Definition:** Collective outliers are groups of data points that collectively deviate significantly from the overall distribution of a dataset.
2. **Characteristics:** Collective outliers may not be outliers when considered individually, but as a group, they exhibit unusual behavior.
3. **Detection:** Techniques for detecting collective outliers include clustering algorithms, density-based methods, and subspace-based approaches.
4. **Impact:** Collective outliers can represent interesting patterns or anomalies in data that may require special attention or further investigation.
5. **Handling:** Handling collective outliers depends on the specific use case and may involve further analysis of the group behavior, identification of contributing factors, or considering contextual information.
6. **Considerations:** Detecting and interpreting collective outliers can be more complex than individual outliers, as the focus is on group behavior rather than individual data points. A proper understanding of the data context and domain knowledge is crucial for the effective handling of collective outliers.

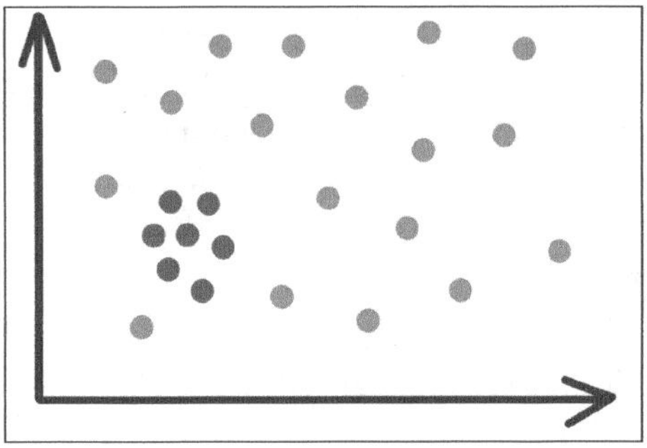

Figure 3.19: *Collective Outlier*

3. Contextual Outliers

1. **Definition:** Contextual outliers are data points that deviate significantly from the expected behavior within a specific context or subgroup.
2. **Characteristics:** Contextual outliers may not be outliers when considered in the entire dataset, but they exhibit unusual behavior within a specific context or subgroup.
3. **Detection:** Techniques for detecting contextual outliers include contextual clustering, contextual anomaly detection, and context-aware machine learning approaches.
4. **Contextual Information:** Contextual information such as time, location, or other relevant factors is crucial in identifying contextual outliers.
5. **Impact:** Contextual outliers can represent unusual or anomalous behavior within a specific context, which may require further investigation or attention.
6. **Handling:** Handling contextual outliers may involve considering the contextual information, contextual normalization or transformation of data, or using context-specific models or algorithms.
7. **Considerations:** Proper understanding of the context and domain-specific knowledge is crucial for accurate detection and interpretation of contextual outliers, as they may vary based on the specific context or subgroup being considered.

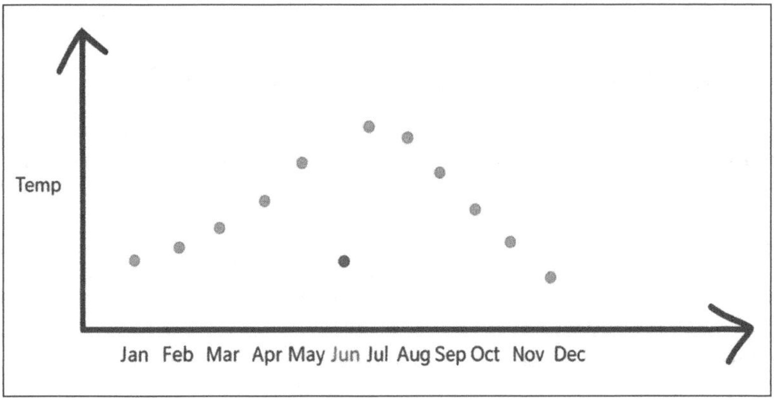

Figure 3.20: *Contextual outlier*

Outlier Detection Methods in Machine Learning

Outlier detection plays a crucial role in ensuring the quality and accuracy of machine learning models. By identifying and removing or handling outliers effectively, we can prevent them from biasing the model, reducing its performance, and hindering its interpretability. Here's an overview of various outlier detection methods:

1. **Statistical Methods**
    - **Z-Score:** This method calculates the standard deviation of the data points and identifies outliers as those with Z-scores exceeding a certain threshold (typically 3 or -3).
    - **Interquartile Range (IQR):** IQR identifies outliers as data points falling outside the range defined by Q1-k*(Q3-Q1) and Q3+k*(Q3-Q1), where Q1 and Q3 are the first and third quartiles, and k is a factor (typically 1.5).
2. **Distance-Based Methods**
    - **K-Nearest Neighbors (KNN):** KNN identifies outliers as data points whose K nearest neighbors are far away from them.
    - **Local Outlier Factor (LOF):** This method calculates the local density of data points and identifies outliers as those with significantly lower density compared to their neighbors.
3. **Clustering-Based Methods**
    - **Density-Based Spatial Clustering of Applications with Noise (DBSCAN):**
    - In DBSCAN, clusters data points based on their density and identifies outliers as points not belonging to any cluster.
    - **Hierarchical clustering:** Hierarchical clustering involves building a hierarchy of clusters by iteratively merging or splitting clusters based on their similarity. Outliers can be identified as clusters containing only a single data point or clusters significantly smaller than others.
4. **Other Methods**
    - **Isolation Forest:** Isolation forest randomly isolates data points by splitting features and identifies outliers as those isolated quickly and easily.
    - **One-class Support Vector Machines (OCSVM):** One-Class SVM learns a boundary around the normal data and identifies outliers as points falling outside the boundary.

Techniques for Handling Outliers in Machine Learning

Outliers, data points that significantly deviate from the majority, can have detrimental effects on machine learning models. To address this, several techniques can be employed to handle outliers effectively:

1. Removal

This involves identifying and removing outliers from the dataset before training the model. Common methods include:

- **Thresholding:** Outliers are identified as data points exceeding a certain threshold (e.g., Z-score > 3).

- **Distance-based methods:** Outliers are identified based on their distance from their nearest neighbors.
- **Clustering:** Outliers are identified as points not belonging to any cluster or belonging to very small clusters.

2. Transformation

This involves transforming the data to reduce the influence of outliers. Common methods include:

- **Scaling:** Standardizing or normalizing the data to have a mean of zero and a standard deviation of one.
- **Winsorization:** Replacing outlier values with the nearest non-outlier value.
- **Log transformation:** Applying a logarithmic transformation to compress the data and reduce the impact of extreme values.

3. Robust Estimation

This involves using algorithms that are less sensitive to outliers. Some examples include:

- **Robust regression:** Algorithms like L1-regularized regression or Huber regression are less influenced by outliers than least squares regression.
- **M-estimators:** These algorithms estimate the model parameters based on a robust objective function that downweights the influence of outliers.
- **Outlier-insensitive clustering algorithms:** Algorithms like DBSCAN are less susceptible to the presence of outliers than K-means clustering.

4. Modeling Outliers

This involves explicitly modeling the outliers as a separate group. This can be done by:

- **Adding a separate feature:** Create a new feature indicating whether a data point is an outlier or not.
- **Using a mixture model:** Train a model that assumes the data comes from a mixture of multiple distributions, where one distribution represents the outliers.

Importance of Outlier Detection in Machine Learning

1. **Biased models:** Outliers can bias a machine learning model towards the outlier values, leading to poor performance on the rest of the data. This can be particularly problematic for algorithms that are sensitive to outliers, such as linear regression.
2. **Reduced accuracy:** Outliers can introduce noise into the data, making it difficult for a machine learning model to learn the true underlying patterns. This can lead to reduced accuracy and performance.
3. **Increased variance:** Outliers can increase the variance of a machine learning model, making it more sensitive to small changes in the data. This can make it difficult to train a stable and reliable model.
4. **Reduced interpretability:** Outliers can make it difficult to understand what a machine learning model has learned from the data. This can make it difficult to trust the model's predictions and can hamper efforts to improve its performance.

Noisy Data

Noisy data are data with a large amount of additional meaningless information called noise. This includes data corruption, and the term is often used as a synonym for corrupt data. It also includes any data that a user system cannot understand and interpret correctly. Many systems, for example, cannot use unstructured text. Noisy data can adversely affect the results of any data analysis and skew conclusions if not handled properly. Statistical analysis is sometimes used to weed the noise out of noisy data.

Noisy data are data that is corrupted, distorted, or has a low signal-to-noise ratio. Improper procedures (or improperly documented procedures) to subtract out the noise in data can lead to a false sense of accuracy or false conclusions.

Data = True Signal + Noise

Noisy data unnecessarily increases the amount of storage space required and can adversely affect any data mining analysis results. Statistical analysis can use information from historical data to weed out noisy data and facilitate data mining. Noisy data can be caused by hardware failures, programming errors, and gibberish input from speech or optical character recognition (OCR) programs. Spelling errors, industry abbreviations, and slang can also impede machine reading. Noise is an unavoidable problem that affects the data collection and preparation processes in Data Mining applications, where errors commonly occur. Noise has two main sources, such as:

1. Implicit errors are introduced by measurement tools, such as different types of sensors.
2. Random errors are introduced by batch processes or experts when the data are gathered, such as in a document digitalization process.

Source of Noise

Differences in real-world measured data from the true values come from multiple factors affecting the measurement.

Random noise is often a large component of the noise in data. Random noise in a signal is measured as the signal-to-noise ratio. Random noise contains almost equal amounts of a wide range of frequencies and is called **white noise** (as colors of light combine to make white). Random noise is an unavoidable problem. It affects the data collection and data preparation processes, where errors commonly occur.

Noise has two main sources:

1. Errors introduced by measurement tools,
2. Random errors are introduced by processing or experts when the data is gathered.

- Improper **filtering** can add noise if the filtered signal is treated as a directly measured signal. For example, Convolution-type digital filters such as a moving average can have side effects such as lags or truncation of peaks. Differentiating digital filters **amplify** random noise in the original data.
- **Outlier** data are data that appear to not belong in the dataset. It can be caused by human error such as transposing numerals, mislabeling, programming bugs, etc. If valid data is identified as an outlier and is mistakenly removed, that also corrupts results. If actual outliers are not removed from the data set, they corrupt the results to a small or large degree, depending on the circumstances.

- **Fraud:** Individuals may deliberately skew data to influence the results toward a desired conclusion. Data that looks good with few outliers reflects well on the individual collecting it, and so there may be an incentive to remove more data as outliers or make the data look smoother than it is.

Types of Noise

A large number of components determine the quality of a dataset. Among them, the class labels and the attribute values directly influence the quality of a classification dataset. The quality of the class labels refers to whether the class of each example is correctly assigned; otherwise, the quality of the attributes refers to their capability of properly characterizing the examples for classification purposes if noise affects attribute values, this capability of characterization and, therefore, the quality of the attributes is reduced. Based on these two information sources, two types of noise can be distinguished in a given dataset.

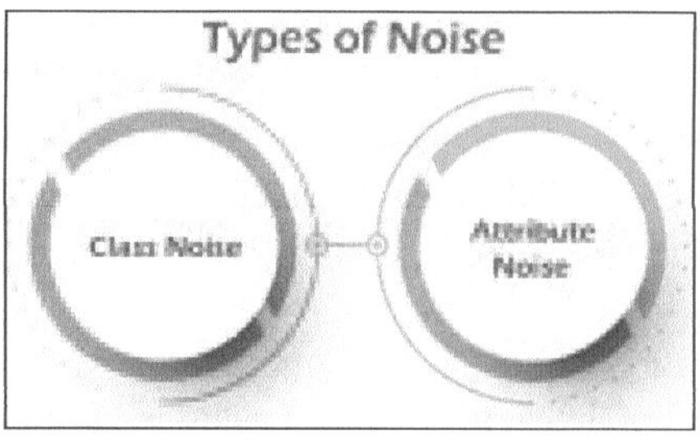

Figure 3.21: *Types of Noise*

1. Class Noise (Label Noise)

This occurs when an example is incorrectly labeled. Class noise can be attributed to several causes, such as subjectivity during the labeling process, data entry errors, or inadequate information used to label each example. Class noise is further divided into two types, such as:

- **Contradictory examples:** Duplicate examples have different class labels. In the figure above, the two examples (0.25, red, class = positive) and (0.25, red, class = negative) are contradictory examples since they have the same attribute values and a different class.
- **Misclassifications examples:** Examples that are labeled as a class different from the real one. The figure placed above the example (0.99, green, class = negative) is a mislabeled example since its class label is wrong, and it would be "positive".

2. Attribute Noise

- **Erroneous attribute values:** In the figure placed above, the example (1.02, green, class = positive) has its first attribute with noise since it has the wrong value.
- **Missing or unknown attribute values:** In the figure placed above, the example(2.05, ? class = negative) has attribute noise since we do not know the value of the second attribute.
- **Incomplete attributes or do not care values:** In the figure placed above, the example (=, green, class = positive) has attribute noise since the value of the first attribute does not affect the rest of the values of the example, including the class of the example.

Considering class and attribute noise as corruptions of the class labels and attribute values, respectively, is common in real-world data. Because of this, these types of noise have also been considered in many works in the literature. For instance, the authors reached a series of interesting conclusions, showing that attribute noise is more harmful than class noise or that eliminating or correcting examples in datasets with class and attribute noise may improve classifier performance. They also showed that attribute noise is more harmful in those attributes highly correlated with the class labels. The authors checked the robustness of methods from different paradigms, such as probabilistic classifiers, decision trees, and instance-based learners or support vector machines, studying the possible causes of their behaviors.

Simulating the Noise of Real-World Datasets

Checking the effect of noisy data on the performance of classifier learning algorithms is necessary to improve their reliability and has motivated the study of how to generate and introduce noise into the data. Three main characteristics can characterize noise generation:

1. The place where the noise is introduced. Noise may affect the input attributes or the output class, impairing the learning process and the resulting model.
2. The noise distribution. How the noise is present can be, for example, uniform or Gaussian.
3. The magnitude of generated noise values. The extent to which the noise affects the dataset can be relative to each data value of each attribute or relative to the minimum, maximum, and standard deviation for each attribute.

The initial amount and type of noise present in real-world datasets are unknown. Therefore, no assumptions about the base noise type and level can be made. For this reason, these datasets are considered noise-free, in the sense that no recognizable noise has been inducted into them. To control the amount of noise in each dataset and check how it affects the classifiers, noise is introduced into each dataset in a supervised manner in the literature.

The two types of noise considered, class and attribute noise, have been modeled using four different noise schemes in the literature; in such a way, the presence of a noise level x% of those types of noise will allow one to simulate the behavior of the classifiers in these scenarios:

1. Class noise usually occurs on the boundaries of the classes, where the examples may have similar characteristics - although it can occur in any other area of the domain. Class noise is introduced in the literature using a uniform class noise scheme (randomly corrupting the class labels of the examples) and a pair-wise class noise scheme (labeling examples of the majority class with the second majority class). Considering these two schemes, noise affects any pair of classes, and only the two majority classes are simulated.
    - **Uniform class noise:** x% of the examples are corrupted. The class labels of these examples are randomly replaced by another one from the other classes.
    - **Pair-wise class noise:** Let X be the majority class and Y the second majority class. An example with the label X has a probability of x/100 of being incorrectly labeled as Y.
2. Attribute noise can proceed from several sources, such as transmission constraints, sensor device faults, sampling irregularities, and transcription errors.

The erroneous attribute values can be unpredictable, i.e., random, or imply a low variation for the correct value. We use the uniform attribute noise scheme and the Gaussian attribute noise scheme to simulate each one of the possibilities, respectively. We introduce attribute noise under the hypothesis that interactions between attributes are weak; consequently, the noise introduced into each attribute has a low correlation with the noise introduced into the rest.

- **Uniform attribute noise:** x% of the values of each attribute in the dataset are corrupted. To corrupt each attribute Ai, x% of the examples in the data set are chosen, and their Ai value is assigned a random value from the domain of the attribute Ai. A uniform distribution is used either for numerical or nominal attributes.
- **Gaussian attribute noise:** This scheme is similar to the uniform attribute noise, but in this case, the Ai values are corrupted, adding a random value to them following a Gaussian distribution of mean = 0 and standard deviation = (max-min)/5, being max and min the limits of the attribute domain. Nominal attributes are treated as in the case of the uniform attribute noise.

How to Manage Noisy Data?

Removing noise from a data set is termed data smoothing. The following ways can be used for Smoothing:

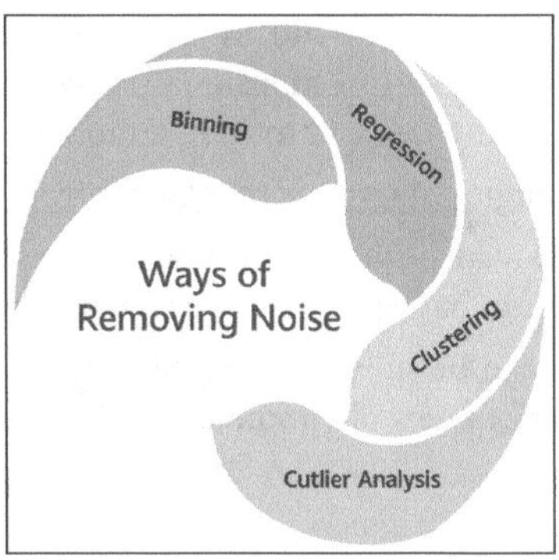

***Figure 3.22:** Ways of removing noise*

1. Binning

Binning is a technique where we sort the data and then partition the data into equal-frequency bins. Then you may either replace the noisy data with the bin mean bin median or the bin boundary. This method is to smooth or handle noisy data. First, the data is sorted, and then the sorted values are separated and stored in the form of bins. There are three methods for smoothing data in the bin.

- **Smoothing by bin mean method:** In this method, the values in the bin are replaced by the mean value of the bin.
- **Smoothing by bin median:** In this method, the values in the bin are replaced by the median value.
- **Smoothing by bin boundary:** In this method, the minimum and maximum values of the bin values are taken, and the closest boundary value replaces the values.

2. Regression

This is used to smooth the data and help handle data when unnecessary data is present. For the analysis, purpose regression helps decide the suitable variable. **Linear regression** refers to finding the best line of between two variables so that one can be used to predict the other. **Multiple linear regression** involves more than two variables. Using regression to find a mathematical equation to fit into the data helps to smooth out the noise.

3. Clustering

This is used for finding the outliers and also in grouping the data. Clustering is generally used in unsupervised learning.

4. Outlier Analysis

Outliers may be detected by clustering, where similar or close values are organized into the same groups or clusters. Thus, values that fall far apart from the cluster may be considered noise or outliers. Outliers are extreme values that deviate from other observations of data. They may indicate variability in measurement, experimental errors, or novelty. In other words, an outlier is an observation that diverges from an overall pattern on a sample. Outliers can be the following kinds, such as:

- **Univariate outliers** can be found when looking at a distribution of values in a single feature space.
- **Multivariate outliers** can be found in an n-dimensional space (of n-features). Looking at distributions in n-dimensional spaces can be very difficult for the human brain. That is why we need to train a model to do it for us.
- **Point outliers** are single data points that lay far from the rest of the distribution.
- **Contextual outliers** can be noise in data, such as punctuation symbols when realizing text analysis or background noise signals when doing speech recognition.
- **Collective outliers** can be subsets of novelties in data, such as a signal that may indicate the discovery of new phenomena.

UNIT 4

Handling Text Data

4.1 BAG OF WORDS

Bag of words can be defined as a Natural Language Processing technique used for text modeling or we can say that it is a method of feature extraction with text data from documents. It involves mainly two things firstly, a vocabulary of known words and, then a measure of the presence of known words. The process of converting NLP text into numbers is called **vectorization** in machine learning language. A lot of different ways are available to convert text into vectors which are:

Counting the number of times each word appears in a document, and Calculating the frequency that each word appears in a document out of all the words in the document.

The bag-of-words model is a way of representing text data when modeling text with machine learning algorithms. The bag-of-words model is simple to understand and implement and has seen great success in problems such as language modelling and document classification.

Bag-of-words is a model for feature extraction in natural language processing.

1. The Problem with Text
2. What is a Bag-of-Words?
3. Example of the Bag-of-Words Model
4. Managing Vocabulary
5. Scoring Words
6. Limitations of Bag-of-Words

The Problem with Text

A problem with modeling text is that it is messy, and techniques like machine learning algorithms prefer well-defined fixed-length inputs and outputs. Machine learning algorithms cannot work with raw text directly; the text must be converted into numbers. Specifically, vectors of numbers.

In language processing, the vectors x are derived from textual data, to reflect various linguistic properties of the text. This is called feature extraction or feature encoding. A popular and simple method of feature extraction with text data is called the bag-of-words model of text.

What is a Bag-of-Words?

A bag-of-words model, or BoW for short, is a way of extracting features from text for use in modeling, such as with machine learning algorithms.

The approach is very simple and flexible and can be used in a myriad of ways for extracting features from documents. A bag of words is a representation of text that describes the occurrence of words within a document. It involves two things:

1. A vocabulary of known words.
2. A measure of the presence of known words.

It is called a "*bag*" of words because any information about the order or structure of words in the document is discarded. The model is only concerned with whether known words occur in the document, not where in the document.

A very common feature extraction procedure for sentences and documents is the bag-of-words approach (BOW). In this approach, we look at the histogram of the words within the text, i.e. considering each word count as a feature. The intuition is that documents are similar if they have similar content. Further, from the content alone we can learn something about the meaning of the document. The bag-of-words can be as simple or complex as you like. The complexity comes both in deciding how to design the vocabulary of known words (or tokens) and how to score the presence of known words.

Example of the Bag-of-Words Model

Step 1: Collect Data

Below is a snippet of the first few lines of text from the book "A Tale of Two Cities" by Charles Dickens, taken from Project Gutenberg.

It was the best of times, it was the worst of times, it was the age of wisdom, it was the age of foolishness, For this small example, let's treat each line as a separate "document" and the 4 lines as our entire corpus of documents.

Step 2: Design the Vocabulary

Now we can make a list of all of the words in our model vocabulary. The unique words here (ignoring case and punctuation) are:

- "it"
- "was"
- "the"
- "best"
- "of"
- "times"
- "worst"
- "age"
- "wisdom"
- "foolishness"

That is a vocabulary of 10 words from a corpus containing 24 words.

Step 3: Create Document Vectors

The next step is to score the words in each document.

The objective is to turn each document of free text into a vector that we can use as input or output for a machine learning model. Because we know the vocabulary has 10 words, we can use a fixed-length document representation of 10, with one position in the vector to score each word.

The simplest scoring method is to mark the presence of words as a boolean value, 0 for absent, 1 for present.

Using the arbitrary ordering of words listed above in our vocabulary, we can step through the first document ("*It was the best of times*") and convert it into a binary vector.

The scoring of the document would look as follows:

- "it" = 1
- "was" = 1
- "the" = 1
- "best" = 1
- "of" = 1
- "times" = 1
- "worst" = 0
- "age" = 0
- "wisdom" = 0
- "foolishness" = 0

As a binary vector, this would look as follows:

```
[1, 1, 1, 1, 1, 1, 0, 0, 0, 0]
```

The other three documents would look as follows:

```
"it was the worst of times" = [1, 1, 1, 0, 1, 1, 1, 0, 0, 0]
"it was the age of wisdom" = [1, 1, 1, 0, 1, 0, 0, 1, 1, 0]
"it was the age of foolishness" = [1, 1, 1, 0, 1, 0, 0, 1, 0, 1]
```

All ordering of the words is nominally discarded and we have a consistent way of extracting features from any document in our corpus, ready for use in modeling. New documents that overlap with the vocabulary of known words, but may contain words outside of the vocabulary, can still be encoded, where only the occurrences of known words are scored and unknown words are ignored.

Managing Vocabulary

As the vocabulary size increases, so does the vector representation of documents. In the previous example, the length of the document vector is equal to the number of known words. You can imagine that for a very large corpus, such as thousands of books, that the length of the vector might be thousands or millions of positions. Further, each document may contain very few of the known words in the vocabulary.

This results in a vector with lots of zero scores, called a sparse vector or sparse representation. Sparse vectors require more memory and computational resources when modeling and the vast number of positions or dimensions can make the modeling process very challenging for traditional algorithms.

As such, there is pressure to decrease the size of the vocabulary when using a bag-of-words model. There are **simple text cleaning** techniques that can be used as a first step, such as:

- Ignoring case
- Ignoring punctuation
- Ignoring frequent words that don't contain much information, called stop words, like "a," "of," etc.
- Fixing misspelled words.
- Reducing words to their stem (e.g. "play" from "playing") using stemming algorithms.

A more sophisticated approach is to create a vocabulary of grouped words. This both changes the scope of the vocabulary and allows the bag-of-words to capture a little bit more meaning from the document.

In this approach, each word or token is called a "gram". Creating a vocabulary of two-word pairs is, in turn, called a bigram model. Again, only the bigrams that appear in the corpus are modeled, not all possible bigrams.

An N-gram is an N-token sequence of words: a 2-gram (more commonly called a bigram) is a two-word sequence of words like "please turn", "turn your", or "your homework", and a 3- gram (more commonly called a trigram) is a three-word sequence of words like "please turn your", or "turn your homework".

For example, the bigrams in the first line of text in the previous section: "It was the best of times" are as follows:

- "it was"
- "was the"
- "the best"
- "best of"
- "of times"

A vocabulary then tracks triplets of words is called a trigram model and the general approach is called the n-gram model, where n refers to the number of grouped words. Often a simple bigram approach is better than a 1-gram bag-of-words model for tasks like documentation classification.

A bag-of-bigrams representation is much more powerful than bag-of-words, and in many cases proves very hard to beat.

Scoring Words

Once a vocabulary has been chosen, the occurrence of words in example documents needs to be scored. In the worked example, we have already seen one very simple approach to scoring: a binary scoring of the presence or absence of words.

Some additional simple scoring methods include:

- **Counts**. Count the number of times each word appears in a document.
- **Frequencies.** Calculate the frequency that each word appears in a document out of all the words in the document.

Word Hashing

You may remember from computer science that a hash function is a bit of math that maps data to a fixed size set of numbers. For example, we use them in hash tables when programming where perhaps names are converted to numbers for fast lookup. We can use a hash representation of known words in our vocabulary. This addresses the problem of having a very large vocabulary for a large text corpus because we can choose the size of the hash space, which is in turn the size of the vector representation of the document.

Words are hashed deterministically to the same integer index in the target hash space. A binary score or count can then be used to score the word. This is called the "*hash trick*" or "feature hashing". The challenge is to choose a hash space to accommodate the chosen vocabulary size to minimize the probability of collisions and trade-off sparsity.

TF-IDF

A problem with scoring word frequency is that highly frequent words start to dominate in the document (e.g. larger score), but may not contain as much "informational content" to the model as rarer but perhaps domain-specific words.

One approach is to rescale the frequency of words by how often they appear in all documents so that the scores for frequent words like "the" that are also frequent across all documents are penalized. This approach to scoring is called Term Frequency – Inverse Document Frequency, or TF-IDF for short, where:

- **Term Frequency**: is a scoring of the frequency of the word in the current document.
- **Inverse Document Frequency**: is a scoring of how rare the word is across documents. The scores are a weighting where not all words are equally as important or interesting.

The scores have the effect of highlighting words that are distinct (contain useful information) in a given document.

Limitations of Bag-of-Words

The bag-of-words model is very simple to understand and implement and offers a lot of flexibility for customization on your specific text data. It has been used with great success on prediction problems like language modeling and documentation classification.

Nevertheless, it suffers from some shortcomings, such as:

- **Vocabulary**: The vocabulary requires careful design, most specifically to manage the size, which impacts the sparsity of the document representations.
- **Sparsity**: Sparse representations are harder to model both for computational reasons (space and time complexity) and also for information reasons, where the challenge is for the models to harness so little information in such a large representational space.
- **Meaning**: Discarding word order ignores the context, and in turn meaning of words in the document (semantics). Context and meaning can offer a lot to the model, that if modeled could tell the difference between the same words differently arranged ("this is interesting" vs "is this interesting"), synonyms ("old bike" vs "used bike"), and much more.

4.2 REGULAR EXPRESSIONS

Regular expressions or Reg Ex is defined as a sequence of characters that are mainly used to find or replace patterns present in the text. In simple words, we can say that a regular expression is a set of characters or a pattern that is used to find substrings in a given string.

A regular expression (RE) is a language for specifying text search strings. It helps us to match or extract other strings or sets of strings, with the help of a specialized syntax present in a pattern. For Example, extracting all hashtags from a tweet, getting email iD or phone numbers, etc from large unstructured text content. Sometimes, we want to identify the different components of an email address.

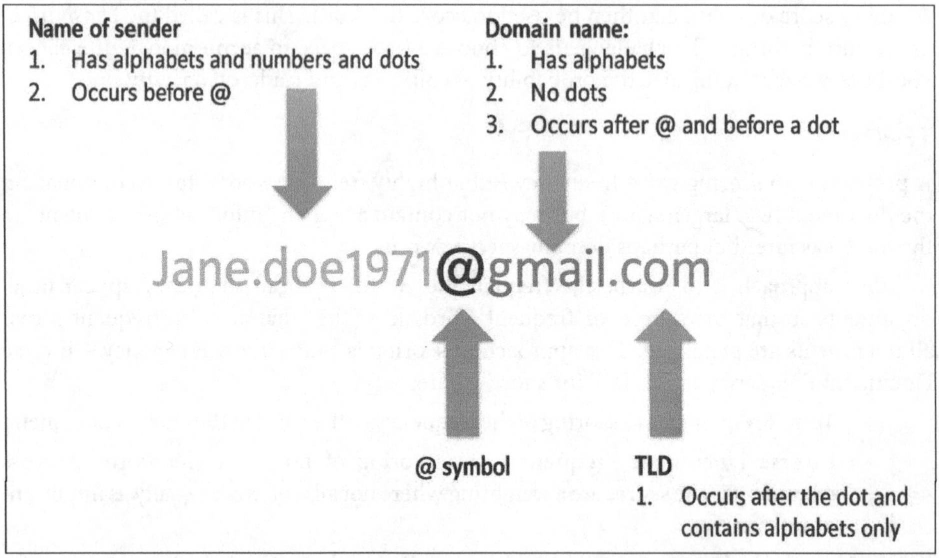

***Figure 4.1:** Different components of an email address*

Simply, a regular expression is defined as an "instruction" that is given to a function on what and how to match, search or replace a set of strings.

Regular Expressions are used in various tasks such as,

- Data pre-processing,
- Rule-based information Mining systems,
- Pattern Matching,
- Text feature Engineering,
- Web scraping,
- Data Extraction, etc.

How do Regular Expressions Work?

Names

Sunil Shyam Ankit Surjeet Sumit Subhi Surbhi Siddharth Sujan

And our goal is to select only those names from the above list that match a certain pattern such as something like this **S u** _ _ _ The names having the first two letters as S and u, followed by only three positions that can be taken up by any of the letters present in the dictionary.

The names **Sunil**, **Sumit,** and **Sujan** fit this criterion as they have S and u in the beginning and three more letters after that. While the rest of the three names do not follow the given criteria. So, the new list extracted is given by,

Extracted Names

Sunil Sumit Sujan

What exactly we have done here is that we have a pattern and a list of student names and we have to find the name that matches the given pattern. That's exactly how regular expressions work.

Properties of Regular Expressions

1. The Regular Expression language is formalized by an American Mathematician named Stephen Cole Kleene.
2. Regular Expression(RE) is a formula in a special language, which can be used for specifying simple classes of strings, a sequence of symbols. In simple words, we can say that Regular Expression is an algebraic notation for characterizing a set of strings.
3. Regular expression requires two things, one is the pattern that we want to search and the other is a corpus of text or a string from which we need to search the pattern.

Mathematically, We can Define The Concept of Regular Expression in the Following Manner

1. ε is a Regular Expression, which indicates that the language is having an empty string.
2. φ is a Regular Expression which denotes that it is an empty language.
3. If X and Y are Regular Expressions, then the following expressions are also regular.
   - X, Y
   - X.Y(Concatenation of XY)
   - X+Y (Union of X and Y)
   - X*, Y* (Kleen Closure of X and Y)
4. If a string is derived from the above rules then that would also be a regular expression.

How can Regular Expressions be Used in NLP?

In NLP, we can use Regular expressions in many places such as,

1. To Validate data fields.

   Examples: dates, email addresses, URLs, abbreviations, etc.
2. To Filter a particular text from the whole corpus.

   Example: spam, disallowed websites, etc.
3. To Identify particular strings in a text.

   Example: token boundaries
4. To convert the output of one processing component into the format required for a second component.

The Concept of Raw String in Regular Expressions

Now let's discuss a crucial concept that you must know while studying Regular Expressions. On the basis of your prior knowledge of Python Programming language, you might know that Python raw string treats backslash() as a literal character.

```
# normal string
path = "C:\desktop\nayan"
print("string:",path)
```

```
string: C:\desktop
ayan
```

In the following example, we have a couple of backslashes present in the string. But in string python treats n as "move to a new line".

After seeing the output, you can observe that n has moved the text after it to a new line. Here "nayan" has become "ayan" and n disappeared from the path. This is not what we want. So, to resolve this issue, now we use the "r" expression to create a raw string:

```
#raw string
path = r"C:\desktop\nayan"
print("raw string:",path)
```

```
raw string: C:\desktop\nayan
```

Again after seeing the output, we have observed that now the entire path has printed out here by simply using "r" in front of the path. Therefore, it is always recommended to use raw string instead of normal string while dealing with Regular expressions.

Common Regex Functions used in NLP

To work with Regular Expressions, Python has a built-in module known as "re". Some common functions from this module are as follows:

- re.search()
- re.match()
- re.sub()
- re.compile()
- re.findall()

re. search( )

This function helps us to detect whether the given regular expression pattern is present in the given input string. It matches the first occurrence of a pattern in the entire string and not just at the beginning. It returns a Regex Object if the pattern is found in the string, else it returns a None object.

Syntax: re.search(patterns, string)

Within search functions, we can use different flags to perform specific operations.

For Example, 're.I' — to ignore the case (either uppercase or lowercase) of the text 're.M' — enables to search the string in multiple lines re.search(pattern, string, flags=re.I | re.M)

```
import re
result = re.search('Founder',r'Kunal Jain is the CEO and Founder of Analytics Vidhya')
print(result.group())
```

```
Founder
```

In the following example, we search for the pattern "founder" in a given string

re.match( )

This function will only match the string if the pattern is present at the very start of the string.

Syntax: re.match(patterns, string)

In the following example, we match a word at the beginning of the string:

```
import re
result = re.match('Analytics',r'Analytics Vidhya is the largest data Scientists community')
print(result)
print(result.group())
```

```
<re.Match object; span=(0, 9), match='Analytics'>
Analytics
```

Here **Pattern** = 'Analytics' and **String** = 'Analytics Vidhya is the largest data Scientists community'. Since the required pattern is present at the beginning of the string we got the matching Object as an output.

And we know that the output of the re.match is an object, so to get the matched expression, we will use the **group()** function of the match object.

As we can observe that we have got our required output using the group() function. Now let us have a look at the other example which presents the second case:

```
import re
result = re.match('Scientists',r'Analytics Vidhya is the largest data Scientists community')
print(result)
```

```
None
```

Here as you can notice, our pattern(Scientists) is not present at the beginning of the string, hence we got **None** as our output.

re.sub( )

This function is used to substitute a substring with another substring.

Syntax: re.sub(patterns, Substitute, Input text)

In the following example, we replace xxx and yyy with abc in the given string:

```
import re
string = "abc xxx abc yyy"
new_string = re.sub(r"xxx|yyy", "abc", string)
print(new_string)
```

```
abc abc abc abc
```

re.compile( )

This function stores the regular expression pattern in the cache memory for faster searches. So, we have to pass the regex pattern to re.compile() function.

```
import re
pattern=re.compile('Analytics')
result1=pattern.findall('Analytics Vidhya teaches Analytics')
print(result1)
result2=pattern.findall('Analytics Vidhya is most popular website for Data Science')
print(result2)
```

```
['Analytics', 'Analytics']
['Analytics']
```

Syntax: re.compile(patterns, repl, string)

re.findall( )

This function will return all the occurrences of the pattern from the string. I would recommend you to always use re.findall(). It can work like both re.search() and re.match(). Therefore, the result of the findall() function is a list of all the matches

```
import re
result = re.findall('founded',r'Andrew NG founded Coursera. He also founded deeplearning.ai')
print(result)
```

```
['founded', 'founded']
```

Syntax: re.findall(patterns, string)

Basics in Regular Expressions

I. **Brackets ([ ]) They are used to specify a disjunction of characters.**

For Examples,

/[cC]hirag/ → Chirag or chirag

/[xyz]/ → 'x', 'y', or 'z'

/[1234567890]/ → any digit

Here slashes represent the start and end of a particular expression.

II. **Dash (-) They are used to specify a range.**

For Examples,

/[A-Z]/ → matches an uppercase letter

/[a-z]/ → matches a lowercase letter

/[0–9]/ → matches a single digit

III. **Caret (^) They can be used for negation or just to mean ^.**

For Examples,

/[ˆa-z]/ → not an lowercase letter

/[ˆCc]/ → neither 'C' nor 'c'

/[ˆ.]/ → not a period

/[cˆ]/ → either 'c' or 'ˆ'

/xˆy/ → the pattern 'xˆy'

IV. Question mark (?) It marks the optionality of the previous expression.

For Examples,

/maths?/ → math or maths

/colou?r/ → color or colour

V. Period (.) Used to specify any character between two expressions.

For Examples,

/beg.n/ → Match any character between which fits between beg and n such as begin, begun

What are Anchors?

These are special characters that help us to perform string operations either at the beginning or at the end of text input. They are used to assert something about the string or the matching process. Generally, they are not used in a specific word or character but are used while we are dealing with more general queries.

Caret Character '^'

It specifies the start of the string. For a string to match the pattern, the character followed by the '^' in the pattern should be the first character of the string.

Dollar Character '$'

It specifies the end of the string. For a string to match the pattern, the character that precedes the '$' in the pattern should be the last character in the string.

For Examples,

^The: Matches a string that starts with 'The' end$: Matches a string that ends with 'end'

^The end$': Exact string match (starts and ends with 'The end') roar: Matches a string that has the text roar in it.

What are Quantifiers?

Some common Quantifiers are: (*, +, ? and { })

They allow us to mention and control over how many times a specific character(s) pattern should occur in the given text.

Character	Regular-expression meaning
.	Any Character, including whitespace or numeric
?	Zero or one of the preceding character
*	Zero or more of the preceding character
+	One or more of the preceding character
^	Negation or complement

For Example, Let's in a given data, we have variations of the word 'Program' such as 'Program', 'Programmed', 'Programmer'. Our goal is to find only those words where one or more occurrences of 'e' appearing in the word 'Program'. So, to achieve our goal, we can use any of the following quantifiers to indicate the presence of a particular character.

Let's discuss all the quantifiers one by one:

'?'

This quantifier matches the preceding character either zero or one time. Generally, It is used to mark the optional presence of a character.

'*'

This quantifier is used to mark the presence of the preceding character either zero or more times.

'+'

This quantifier matches the preceding character either one or more times. That means for the pattern to match the string, the preceding character has to be Present at least once.

{m,n} quantifier

i. {m, n}

This quantifier matches the preceding character from 'm' number of times to 'n' number of times.

ii. {m, }

This quantifier matches the preceding character from 'm' number of times infinite times, therefore, there is no upper limit on the occurrence of the preceding character.

iii. {, n}

This quantifier matches the preceding character from zero to 'n' a number of times, therefore, the upper limit is fixed for the occurrence of the preceding character.

iv. {n}

This quantifier matches if the preceding character occurs exactly 'n' number of times.

Each of the earlier mentioned quantifiers can be written in the form of {m,n} quantifier in the following way:

- '?' is equivalent to zero or once, or {0, 1}
- '*' is equivalent to zero or more times, or {0, }
- '+' is equivalent to one or more times, or {1, }

For Examples,

abc*: matches a string that has 'ab' followed by zero or more 'c'.

abc+: matches 'ab' followed by one or more 'c'

abc?: matches 'ab' followed by zero or one 'c'

abc{2}: matches 'ab' followed by 2 'c'

abc{2, }: matches 'ab' followed by 2 or more 'c'

abc{2, 5}: matches 'ab' followed by 2 upto 5 'c'

a(bc)*: matches 'a' followed by zero or more copies of the sequence 'bc' Whitespace

A white space can include a single space, multiple spaces, tab space, or a newline character (also known as a vertical space). It will match the corresponding spaces in the string.

For Examples,

' +', i.e. a space followed by a plus sign will match one or more spaces.

'Chirag Goyal' will allow you to look for the name 'Chirag Goyal' in any given string.

Pipe Operator

It's denoted by '|'. It is used as an OR operator. We have to use it inside the parentheses.

For Example, Consider the pattern **'(play|walk)ed'** –

The above pattern will match both the strings — 'played' and 'walked'.

Therefore, the pipe operator tells us about the place inside the parentheses that can be either of the strings or the characters.

Wildcard Character

The '.' (dot) character is also known as the wildcard character. It acts as a placeholder and can match any of the characters.

For Example, if a string starts with three characters, followed by two 0s and three 1s, followed by any four characters. Then, the valid strings that follow the above condition can be

Escaping Special Characters

The characters which we discussed above in quantifiers such as '?', '*', '+', '(', ')', '{', etc. can also appear in the input text. So, In such cases to extract these specific characters, we have to use the escape sequences.

The escape sequence, represented by a backslash '', is used to escape the special meaning of the special characters.

*

t is used to escape the star

.

It is used to escape the dot

+

It is used to escape the plus sign (to match a '+' sign)

?

It is used to escape the question mark (to match a question mark)

The '' itself is a special character, and to match the '' character, we have to use the pattern ' \' to escape the backslash.

Character Sets

1. Character sets provide a lot more flexibility than just typing a wildcard or the literal characters. These are groups of characters specified inside square brackets.
2. Character sets can be specified with or without the help of a quantifier.
3. When no quantifier succeeds the character set, it matches only one character and the match is successful only if the character in the string is one of the characters present inside the character set.

For Examples,

- **Example-1:** The pattern **'[a-z]ed'** will match strings such as 'ted', 'bed', 'red' and so on because the first character of each string — 't', 'b' and 'r' — is present inside the range of the character set.
- **Example-2:** When we use a character set with a quantifier, such as **'[a-z]+ed'**, it will match only those words that end with 'ed' like 'watched', 'baked', 'jammed', 'educated', and so on.

From the above examples, we have observed that when a quantifier is present inside the character set, then it loses its special meaning and is treated as a normal character..

Let's discuss the two use cases of '^' :

- **Outside a character set:** works as an anchor
- **Inside a character set:** works as a complement operator, i.e. matches any character other than the ones mentioned inside the character set.

For Example, The pattern **[0–9]** matches any single-digit number but on the contrary, the pattern **'[^ 0-9]'** matches any single-digit character that is not a digit.

Meta Sequences

Special Sequences	
\b	Word Boundary (Zero width)
\d	Any Decimal digit(equivalent to[0-9])
\D	Any non-digit character(equivalent to[^0-9])
\s	Anynon-whitespace character(equivalent to [\t\n\r\f\v])
\S	Any non-white space character(equivalent to [^\t\nr\f\v])
\w	Any non-alphanumeric character(equivalent to [a-zA-Z0-9_]
\W	Any non- alphanumeric character(equivalent to [^ a-zA-Z0-9_])

Meta Sequences are a shorthand way to write commonly used character sets in the form of regular expressions. The commonly used meta-sequences are as follows:

We can use meta-sequences in the following two different ways: Use them without the square brackets.

For Example, the pattern 'w+' will match any alphanumeric character. Use them inside the square brackets.

For Example, the pattern '[w]+' is the same as 'w+'.

4.3 SENTENCE SPLITTING AND TOKENIZATION

Splitting Text into Sentences

Splitting textual data into sentences can be considered as an easy task, where a text can be splitted to sentences by '.' or '/n' characters. However, in free text data this pattern is not consistent, and authors can break a line in the middle of the sentence or use "." in wrong places. This phenomenon is common in medical visits summary texts and conversational/messaging texts for example.

To overcome this and in order to develop a generic model that can be used in any language, a deep learning model is used that decides if two sentences need to be merged.

First, split the text by all common characters, '.' and '/n' for example, and then given two sentences the model will decide if they have to be merged or not. Thus, the model will give a new division of the text into sentences.

Creating the Dataset

To create the dataset for training consider a list of articles/ cases/ conversations, for example, consider a list of articles. Let us define a positive pair as a pair of sentences that should be splitted and remain two different sentences with "." between them. A negative pair is a pair of sentences that should be merged and considered as one sentence, with no '.' between them.

Create **positive pairs** using *nltk.sent_tokenize* function, splitting the text by '.', which is true for most of the cases and will let the model to learn the mechanism and role of the '.' character.

Create **negative pairs** by splitting sentences in the middle, meaning we don't want to split the sentence. we use the *min_sentence_length_for_splitting* parameter to define the minimum length of sentences that we would like to split for the negative pairs (we don't want to split too short sentences). A code example for creating the dataset:

```
from typing importList
import numpy as np import nltk
from itertools import chain nltk.download('punkt')
def create_dataset(texts: List[str], min_sentence_length_for_splitting=10): ''' Create positives and negatives pairs of sentences.
Positive pair is a pair of sentences that should be splitted, using nltk.sent_tokenize (without \n).
Negative pair is a sentence that we split in the middle '''
positives_pairs = [] negative_pairs = []
```

For Text in Texts

```
sentences = nltk.sent_tokenize(text) if len(sentences)>1:
sentences = [nltk.tokenize.word_tokenize(sentence.replace('.', '')) for sentence in sentences: sentences_pairs = list(zip(sentences[:-1], sentences[1:])) positives_pairs. append(sentences_pairs)
```

For Negative_sample in Sentences

```
if len(negative_sample) > min_sentence_length_for_splitting: first_sent, second sent = negative_sample[:len(negative_sample)] negative_sample[len(negative_sample)] negative_pairs.append([(first_sent, second_sent)])
positives_pairs = list(chain.from_iterable(positives_pairs)) negative_pairs = list(chain.from_iterable(negative_pairs)) return positives_pairs, negative_pairs
```

Example of a Positive Pair

```
[ 'Group', 'members', ' have', 'played', 'around', 'the', 'United', 'States', 'and', 'in', 'New'.zealand']
['Other', 'teams', 'are', 'forming', 'around', 'the', 'world']
```

Example of a Negative Pair

['Common', 'examples', 'include', 'the', 'chamber', 'tools', 'and', 'other']

['megalithic', 'monuments', 'and', 'the', 'vertical', 'elements', 'of', 'the', 'trilithons', 'at', 'Stonehenge']

We trained a deep learning model that takes as an input the two sentences. For the first sentence we apply a forward LSTM layer and for the second sentence we apply a backward LSTM layer. We use one forward layer and one backward layer in order to predict if we should have a "." in the middle, so we expect the forward pass of the first sentence to embed a pattern of an end of first sentence and the backward pass of the second sentence to embed a pattern of a beginning of second sentence.

Then we concatenate both embeddings to represent the ending and beginning meaning of the two sentences in order to predict if they should be splitted or not (should have a "." between them or not).

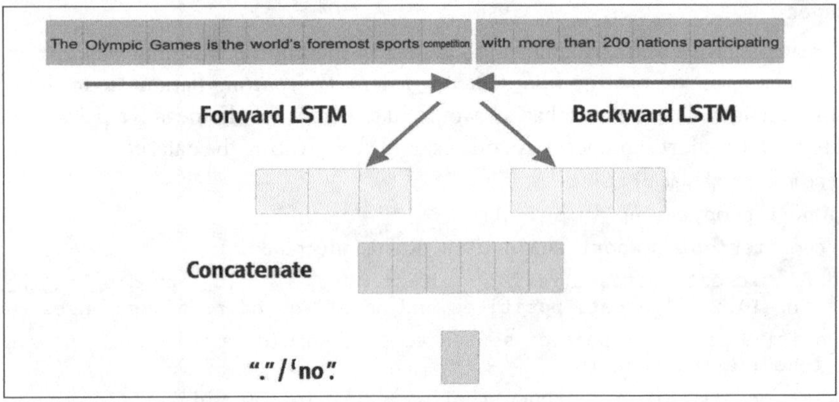

Figure 4.2: LSTM Layer

Tokenization

Tokenization breaks text into smaller parts for easier machine analysis, helping machines understand human language.

Tokenization, in the realm of Natural Language Processing (NLP) and **machine learning**, refers to the process of converting a sequence of text into smaller parts, known as tokens. These tokens can be as small as characters or as long as words. The primary reason this process matters is that it helps machines understand human language by breaking it down into bite-sized pieces, which are easier to analyze.

Tokenization Explained

Instead of diving straight into complex paragraphs, you'd start by introducing them to individual letters, then syllables, and finally, whole words. In a similar vein, tokenization breaks down vast stretches of text into more digestible and understandable units for machines.

The primary goal of tokenization is to represent text in a manner that's meaningful for machines without losing its context. By converting text into tokens, algorithms can more easily identify patterns. This pattern recognition is crucial because it makes it possible for machines to understand and respond to human input. For instance, when a machine encounters the word "running", it doesn't see it as a singular entity but rather as a combination of tokens that it can analyze and derive meaning from.

To delve deeper into the mechanics, consider the sentence, "Chatbots are helpful." When we tokenize this sentence by words, it transforms into an array of individual words:

["Chatbots", "are", "helpful"].

This is a straightforward approach where spaces typically dictate the boundaries of tokens. However, if we were to tokenize by characters, the sentence would fragment into:

["C", "h", "a", "t", "b", "o", "t", "s", " ", "a", "r", "e", " ", "h", "e", "l", "p", "f", "u", "l"].

This character-level breakdown is more granular and can be especially useful for certain languages or specific NLP tasks.

In essence, tokenization is akin to dissecting a sentence to understand its anatomy. NLP practitioners use tokenization to dissect and understand the structure and meaning of text.

Types of Tokenization

Tokenization methods vary based on the granularity of the text breakdown and the specific requirements of the task at hand. These methods can range from dissecting text into individual words to breaking them down into characters or even smaller units.

- **Word tokenization:** This method breaks text down into individual words. It's the most common approach and is particularly effective for languages with clear word boundaries like English.
- **Character tokenization:** Here, the text is segmented into individual characters. This method is beneficial for languages that lack clear word boundaries or for tasks that require a granular analysis, such as spelling correction.
- **Subword tokenization**: Striking a balance between word and character tokenization, this method breaks text into units that might be larger than a single character but smaller than a full word. For instance, "Chatbots" could be tokenized into "Chat" and "bots". This approach is especially useful for languages that form meaning by combining smaller units or when dealing with out-of- vocabulary words in NLP tasks.

The True Reasons behind Tokenization

As tokens are the building blocks of Natural Language, the most common way of processing the raw text happens at the token level.

For example, transformer-based models – the State of The Art (SOTA) Deep Learning architectures in NLP – process the raw text at the token level. Similarly, the most popular deep learning architectures for NLP like RNN, GRU, and LSTM also process the raw text at the token level.

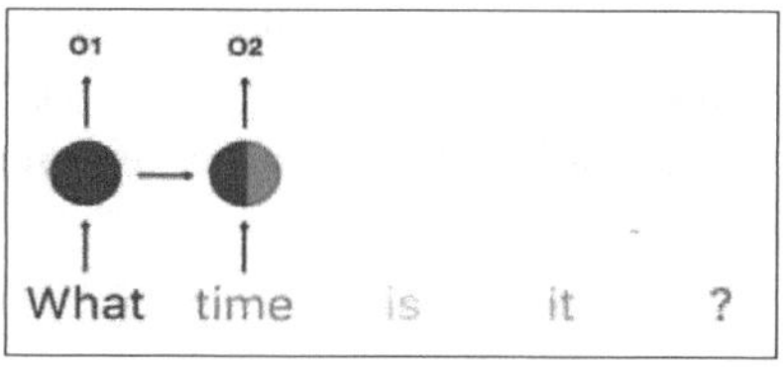

Figure 4.3: *Tokenization*

Hence, Tokenization is the foremost step while modeling text data. Tokenization is performed on the corpus to obtain tokens. The following tokens are then used to prepare a vocabulary.

Vocabulary refers to the set of unique tokens in the corpus. Remember that vocabulary can be constructed by considering each unique token in the corpus or by considering the top K Frequently Occurring Words.

Creating Vocabulary is the Ultimate Goal of Tokenization

One of the simplest hacks to boost the performance of the NLP model is to create a vocabulary out of top K frequently occurring words.

Now, let's understand the usage of the vocabulary in Traditional and Advanced Deep Learning- based NLP methods.

Traditional NLP approaches such as Count Vectorizer and TF-IDF use vocabulary as features. Each word in the vocabulary is treated as a unique feature:

	1	Play	Cricket	Football	Tennis
Doc 1	1	1	1	1	1
Doc 2	1	1	0	1	0
Doc 3	0	1	1	0	0
Doc 4	1	1	0	0	1

Traditional NLP: Count Vectorizer

- In Advanced Deep Learning-based NLP architectures, vocabulary is used to create the tokenized input sentences. Finally, the tokens of these sentences are passed as inputs to the model

Word Tokenization

Word Tokenization is the most commonly used tokenization algorithm. It splits a piece of text into individual words based on a certain delimiter. Depending upon delimiters, different word-level tokens are formed. Pre-trained Word Embeddings such as Word2Vec and GloVe come under word tokenization.

Drawbacks of Word Tokenization

1. One of the major issues with word tokens is dealing with **Out Of Vocabulary (OOV) words**. OOV words refer to the new words which are encountered at testing. These new words do not exist in the vocabulary. Hence, these methods fail in handling OOV words.
   - A small trick can rescue word tokenizers from OOV words. The trick is to form the vocabulary with the Top K Frequent Words and replace the rare words in training data with **unknown tokens (UNK)**. This helps the model to learn the representation of OOV words in terms of UNK tokens
   - So, during test time, any word that is not present in the vocabulary will be mapped to a UNK token. This is how we can tackle the problem of OOV in word tokenizers.

- The problem with this approach is that the entire information of the word is lost as we are mapping OOV to UNK tokens. The structure of the word might be helpful in representing the word accurately. And another issue is that every OOV word gets the same representation.

2. Another issue with word tokens is connected to the size of the vocabulary. Generally, pre-trained models are trained on a large volume of the text corpus. So, just imagine building the vocabulary with all the unique words in such a large corpus. This explodes the vocabulary! This leads to Character tokenization.

Character Tokenization

Character Tokenization splits apiece of text into a set of characters. It overcomes the drawbacks we saw above about Word Tokenization.

- Character Tokenizers handles OOV words coherently by preserving the information of the word. It breaks down the OOV word into characters and represents the word in terms of these characters
- It also limits the size of the vocabulary. Want to talk a guess on the size of the vocabulary? 26 since the vocabulary contains a unique set of characters

Drawbacks of Character Tokenization

Character tokens solve the OOV problem but the length of the input and output sentences increases rapidly as we are representing a sentence as a sequence of characters. As a result, it becomes challenging to learn the relationship between the characters to form meaningful words. This brings us to another tokenization known as Subword Tokenization which is in between a Word and Character tokenization.

Subword Tokenization

Subword Tokenization splits the piece of text into subwords (or n-gram characters). For example, words like lower can be segmented as low-er, smartest as smart-est, and so on. Transformed-based models – the SOTA in NLP – rely on Subword Tokenization algorithms for preparing vocabulary. Let us discuss one of the most popular Subword Tokenization algorithms known as Byte Pair Encoding (BPE).

Byte Pair Encoding (BPE)

Byte Pair Encoding (BPE) is a widely used tokenization method among transformer-based models. BPE addresses the issues of Word and Character Tokenizers:

- BPE tackles OOV effectively. It segments OOV as subwords and represents the word in terms of these subwords
- The length of input and output sentences after BPE are shorter compared to character tokenization

BPE is a word segmentation algorithm that merges the most frequently occurring character or character sequences iteratively. Here is a step by step guide to learn BPE.

Steps to Learn BPE

1. Split the words in the corpus into characters after appending </w>
2. Initialize the vocabulary with unique characters in the corpus

3. Compute the frequency of a pair of characters or character sequences in corpus
4. Merge the most frequent pair in corpus
5. Save the best pair to the vocabulary
6. Repeat steps 3 to 5 for a certain number of iterations We will understand the steps with an example.

1. Consider a Corpus

Corpus

low	lower	newest
low	lower	newest
low	widest	newest
low	widest	newest
low	widest	newest

(a) Append the End of the Word (Say </W>) Symbol to Every Word in the Corpus

Corpus

low</w>	lower</w>	newest</w>
low</w>	lower</w>	newest</w>
low</w>	widest</w>	newest</w>
low</w>	widest</w>	newest</w>
low</w>	widest</w>	newest</w>

(b) Tokenize Words in a Corpus Into Characters

Corpus

l o w </w>	l o w e r </w>	n e w e s t </w>
l o w </w>	l o w e r </w>	n e w e s t </w>
l o w </w>	w i d e s t </w>	n e w e s t </w>
l o w </w>	w i d e s t</w>	n e w e s t </w>
l o w </w>	w i d e s t </w>	n e w e s t </w>

2. Intialize the Vocabulary

Vocabulary

d	e	i	l	n	o	s	t	w

Iteration 1

3. Compute Frequency

Frequency

d-e (3)	l-o (7)	t-</w> (8)
e-r (2)	n-e (5)	w-</w> (5)
e-s (8)	o-w (7)	w-e (7)
e-w (5)	r-</w> (2)	w-i (3)
i-d (3)	s-t (8)	

4. Merge the Most Frequent Pair

Corpus

l o w </w>	l o w e r </w>	n e w es t </w>
l o w </w>	l o w e r </w>	n e w es t </w>
l o w </w>	w i d es t </w>	n e w es t </w>
l o w </w>	w i d es t </w>	n e w es t </w>
l o w </w>	w i d es t </w>	n e w es t </w>

5. Save the Best Pair

Vocabulary

d	e	i	l	n	o	s	t	w
es								

Repeat steps 3-5 for every iteration from now. Let me illustrate for one more iteration.

Iteration 2

3. Compute Frequency

Frequency

d-es (3)	l-o (7)	w-</w> (5)
e-r (2)	n-e (5)	w-es (5)
e-w (5)	o-w (7)	w-e (2)
es-t (8)	r-</w> (2)	w-i (3)
i-d (3)	t-</w> (8)	

4. Merge the most Frequent Pair

Corpus		
l o w </w>	l o w e r </w>	n e w est </w>
l o w </w>	l o w e r </w>	n e w est </w>
l o w </w>	w i d est </w>	n e w est </w>
l o w </w>	w i d est </w>	n e w est </w>
l o w </w>	w i d est </w>	n e w est </w>

5. Save the Best Pair

Vocabulary

d	e	i	l	n	o	s	t	w
[illegible]	[illegible]							

6. After 10 Iterations, Bpe Merge Operations Looks Like

Vocabulary

d	e	i	l	n	o	s	t	w
[illegible]	[illegible]	[illegible]	[illegible]	[illegible]	[illegible]	[illegible]	[illegible]	[illegible]

Applying BPE to OOV Words

At test time, the OOV word is split into sequences of characters. Then the learned operations are applied to merge the characters into larger known symbols. Here is a step-by-step procedure for representing OOV words:

1. Split the OOV word into characters after appending </w>
2. Compute pair of character or character sequences in a word
3. Select the pairs present in the learned operations
4. Merge the most frequent pair
5. Repeat steps 2 and 3 until merging is possible

Tokenization Use Cases

Tokenization serves as the backbone for a myriad of applications in the digital realm, enabling machines to process and understand vast amounts of text data. By breaking down text into manageable chunks, tokenization facilitates more efficient and accurate **data analysis**. Here are some prominent use cases where tokenization plays a pivotal role:

- **Search engines.** When you type a query into a search engine like Google, it employs tokenization to dissect your input. This breakdown helps the engine sift through billions of documents to present you with the most relevant results.

- **Machine translation.** Tools such as Google Translate utilize tokenization to segment sentences in the source language. Once tokenized, these segments can be translated and then reconstructed in the target language, ensuring the translation retains the original context.
- **Speech recognition.** Voice-activated assistants like Siri or Alexa rely heavily on tokenization. When you pose a question or command, your spoken words are first converted into text. This text is then tokenized, allowing the system to process and act upon your request.

Tokenization Challenges

- **Ambiguity:** Language is inherently ambiguous. Consider the sentence "Flying planes can be dangerous." Depending on how it's tokenized and interpreted, it could mean that the act of piloting planes is risky or that planes in flight pose a danger. Such ambiguities can lead to vastly different interpretations.
- **Languages without clear boundaries:** Some languages, like Chinese or Japanese, don't have clear spaces between words, making tokenization a more complex task. Determining where one word ends and another begins can be a significant challenge in such languages.
- **Handling special characters:** Texts often contain more than just words. Email addresses, URLs, or special symbols can be tricky to tokenize. For instance, should "john.doe@email.com" be treated as a single token or split at the period or the "@" symbol?

Advanced tokenization methods, such as context-aware tokenizers like the BERT tokenizer, have been developed to handle such ambiguities. For languages without clear word boundaries, character or subword tokenization can offer a more effective approach.

Additionally, predefined rules and regular expressions can assist in handling special characters and complex strings.

Implementing Tokenization

The landscape of Natural Language Processing offers a plethora of tools, each tailored to specific needs and complexities.

Here's a guide to some of the most prominent tools and methodologies available for tokenization:

- **NLTK (Natural Language Toolkit):** A stalwart in the NLP community, NLTK is a comprehensive Python library that caters to a wide range of linguistic needs. It offers both word and sentence tokenization functionalities, making it a versatile choice for beginners and seasoned practitioners alike.
- **Spacy:** A modern and efficient alternative to NLTK, Spacy is another Python-based NLP library. It boasts speed and supports multiple languages, making it a favorite for large-scale applications.
- **BERT tokenizer:** Emerging from the BERT pre-trained model, this tokenizer excels in context-aware tokenization. It's adept at handling the nuances and ambiguities of language, making it a top choice for advanced NLP projects (see this tutorial on NLP with BERT).

Advanced Techniques

- **Byte-Pair Encoding (BPE):** An adaptive tokenization method, BPE tokenizes based on the most frequent byte pairs in a text. It's particularly effective for languages that form meaning by combining smaller units.
- **Sentence Piece:** An unsupervised text tokenizer and detokenize mainly for Neural Network- based text generation tasks. It handles multiple languages with a single model and can tokenize text into subwords, making it versatile for various NLP tasks.

4.4 STOPWORDS

Stopwords are the most common words in any natural language. To analyze text data and build NLP models, these stopwords might not add much value to the meaning of the document.

Generally, the most common words used in a text are "the", "is", "in", "for", "where", "when", "to", "at" etc.

Consider this text string – "There is a pen on the table". Now, the words "is", "a", "on", and "the" add no meaning to the statement while parsing it. Whereas words like "there", "book", and "table" are the keywords and tell us what the statement is all about.

Why do we Need to Remove Stop words?

Removing stop words is not a hard and fast rule in NLP. It depends upon the task that we are working on. For tasks like text classification, where the text is to be classified into different categories, stop words are removed or excluded from the given text so that more focus can be given to those words that define the meaning of the text.

Here are a few key benefits of removing stop words:

- On removing stopwords, dataset size decreases and the time to train the model also decreases
- Removing stopwords can potentially help improve the performance as there are fewer and only meaningful tokens left. Thus, it could increase classification accuracy
- Even search engines like Google remove stopwords for fast and relevant retrieval of data from the database

When Should we Remove Stopwords?

Remove Stopwords

We can remove stopwords while performing the following tasks:

- Text Classification
- Spam Filtering
- Language Classification
- Genre Classification
- Caption Generation
- Auto-Tag Generation

Avoid Stop Word Removal

- Machine Translation
- Language Modeling
- Text Summarization
- Question-Answering problems

Different Methods to Remove Stopwords

1. Stopword Removal Using NLTK

NLTK, or the Natural Language Toolkit, is a treasure trove of a library for text preprocessing. It's one of my favorite Python libraries. **NLTK has a list of stopwords stored in 16 different languages.**

You can use the below code to see the list of stopwords in NLTK:

```
import nltk
from nltk.corpus import stopwords
 set(stopwords.words('english'))
```

Now, to remove stopwords using NLTK, you can use the following code block. Here is the list we obtained after tokenization:

```
He determined to drop his litigation with the monastry, and relinguish his claims to the wood-cutting and fishery rights at once. He was the more ready to do this because the rights had become much less valuable, and he had indeed the vaguest idea where the wood and river in question were.
```

And the list after removing stop words: The size of the text has almost reduced to half.

```
He determined drop litigation monastry, relinguish claims wood-cutting fishery rights. He ready because rights become much less valuable, indeed vaguest idea wood river question.
```

2. Stopword Removal using spaCy

spaCy is one of the most versatile and widely used libraries in NLP. We can quickly and efficiently remove stopwords from the given text using SpaCy. It has a list of its own stopwords that can be imported as **STOP_WORDS** from the **spacy.lang.en.stop_words** class. Here's how you can remove stopwords using spaCy in Python:

from spacy.lang.en import English

Load English tokenizer, tagger, parser, NER and word vectors nlp = English()

text = """"He determined to drop his litigation with the monastry, and relinguish his claims to the wood-cuting and fishery rights at once. He was the more ready to do this because the rights had become much less valuable, and he had indeed the vaguest idea where the wood and river in question were.""""

#"nlp" Object is used to create documents with linguistic annotations. my_doc = nlp(text)

Create list of word tokens token_list = []

for token in my_doc: token_list.append(token.text)

from spacy.lang.en.stop_words import STOP_WORDS

Create list of word tokens after removing stopwords filtered_sentence =[]

```
He determined to drop his litigation with the monastry and relinguish his claims to the wood-cuting and \n fishery rights at once. He was the more ready to do this because the rights had become much less valuable, and he had \n indeed the vaguest idea where the wood and river in question were.
```

And the list after removing stopwords:

```
determined drop litigation monastry, relinguish claims wood-cuting \n fishery rihgts. ready becuase rights become valuable, \n vaguest idea wood river question.
```

An important point to note – stopword removal doesn't take off the punctuation marks or newline characters. We will need to remove them manually.

3. Stopword Removal Using Gensim

Gensim is a pretty handy library to work with on NLP tasks. While pre-processing, gensim provides methods to remove stopwords as well. We can easily import the **remove_stopwords** method from the class **gensim.parsing.preprocessing.**

```
He determined drop litigation monastry, relinguish claims wood-cuting fishery rihgts once. He ready becuase rights valuable, vaguest idea wood river question were.
```

While using gensim for removing stopwords, we can directly use it on the raw text. There's no need to perform tokenization before removing stopwords. This can save us a lot of time.

4.5 INTRODUCTION TO TEXT NORMALIZATION

In any natural language, words can be written or spoken in more than one form depending on the situation. That's what makes the language such a thrilling part of our lives, right? For example:

- Lisa **ate** the food and washed the dishes.
- They were **eating** noodles at a cafe.
- Don't you want to **eat** before we leave?
- We have just **eaten** our breakfast.
- It also **eats** fruit and vegetables.

In all these sentences, we can see that the word **eat** has been used in multiple forms. For us, it is easy to understand that eating is the activity here. So it doesn't really matter to us whether it is 'ate', 'eat', or 'eaten' – we know what is going on.

Unfortunately, that is not the case with machines. They treat these words differently. Therefore, we need to normalize them to their root word, which is "eat" in our example.

Hence, **text normalization** is a process of transforming a word into a single canonical form. This can be done by two processes, **stemming** and **lemmatization**. Let's understand what they are in detail.

What are Stemming and Lemmatization?

Stemming and Lemmatization is simply normalization of words, which means reducing a word to its root form. In most natural languages, a root word can have many variants. For example, the word 'play' can be used as 'playing', 'played', 'plays', etc. You can think of similar examples (and there are plenty).

Stemming

- Stemming is a text normalization technique that cuts off the end or beginning of a word by taking into account a list of common prefixes or suffixes that could be found in that word
- It is a rudimentary rule-based process of stripping the suffixes ("ing", "ly", "es", "s" etc) from a word

Lemmatization

Lemmatization, on the other hand, is an organized & step-by-step procedure of obtaining the root form of the word. It makes use of vocabulary (dictionary importance of words) and morphological analysis (word structure and grammar relations).

Why do we need to Perform Stemming or Lemmatization?

Let's consider the following two sentences:

- He was driving
- He went for a drive

We can easily state that both sentences convey the same meaning, that is, driving activity in the past. A machine will treat both sentences differently. Thus, to make the text understandable for the machine, we need to perform stemming or lemmatization. Another benefit of text normalization is that it reduces the number of unique words in the text data. This helps in bringing down the training time of the machine learning model (and don't we all want that?).

Stemming algorithm works by cutting the suffix or prefix from the word. **Lemmatization** is a more powerful operation as it takes into consideration the morphological analysis of the word. Lemmatization returns the lemma, which is the root word of all its inflection forms.

We can say that stemming is a quick and dirty method of chopping off words to its root form while on the other hand, lemmatization is an intelligent operation that uses dictionaries which are created by in-depth linguistic knowledge. **Hence, Lemmatization helps in forming better features.**

Methods to Perform Text Normalization

1. Text Normalization Using NLTK

The NLTK library has a lot of amazing methods to perform different steps of data preprocessing. There are methods like *PorterStemmer()* and *WordNetLemmatizer()* to perform stemming and lemmatization, respectively.

Stemming

```
from nltk.corpus import stopwords
from nltk.tokenize import word_tokenize from nltk.stem import PorterStemmer
```

```
    stop_words = set(stopwords.words('english'))
    word_tokens = word_tokenize(text)
    filtered_sentence = [] for w in word_tokens:
    if w not in stop_words:
    Stem_words = []
    ps =PorterStemmer()
    for w in filtered_sentence:
    rootWord=ps.stem(w) Stem_words.append(rootWord) print(filtered_sentence)
print(Stem_words)
```

He determined drop litigation monastery, relinquish claims wood-cutting fishery rights. He ready because rights become much less valuable, indeed vaguest idea wood river question. He determin drop litig monastri, relinguish claim wood-cut fisheri right. He readi becaus right become much less valuabl, inde vaguest idea wood river question

Lemmatization

```
        from nltk.corpus import stopwords
        from nltk.tokenize import word_tokenize import nltk
        from nltk.stem import WordNetLemmatizer
        set(stopwords.words('english'))
    text = """He determined to drop his litigation with the monastry, and relinguish his claims to the wood-cuting and fishery rihgts at once . He was the more ready to do this becuase the rights had become much less valuable, and he had indeed the vaguest idea where the wood and river in question were."""
    stop_words = set(stopwords.words('english'))
    word_tokens = word_tokenize(text) filtered_sentence = []
    for w in word_tokens:
    if w not in stop_words:
    filtered_sentence.append(w)
    print(filtered_sentence) lemma_word = []
    import nltk
    from nltk.stem import WordNetLemmatizer
    wordnet_lemmatizer = WordNetLemmatizer() for w in filtered_sentence:
    word1 = wordnet_lemmatizer.lemmatize(w, pos = "n") word2 =
    wordnet_lemmatizer.lemmatize(word1, pos = "v") word3 =
    wordnet_lemmatizer.lemmatize(word2, pos = ("a")) lemma_word.append(word3)
    print(lemma_word)
```

He determined drop litigation monastry, relinguish claims wood-cuting fishery rihgts. He ready becuase rights become much less valuable, indeed vaguest idea wood river question. He determined drop litigation monastry, relinguish claim wood-cuting fishery rihgts. He ready becuase right become much le valuable, indeed vaguest idea wood river question.

Here, **v** stands for **verb**, **a** stands for **adjective** and **n** stands for **noun**. The lemmatizer only lemmatizes those words which match the **pos** parameter of the lemmatize method.

Lemmatization is done on the basis of part-of-speech tagging (POS tagging). We'll talk in detail about POS tagging in an upcoming article.

2. Text Normalization using spaCy

spaCy, as we saw earlier, is an amazing NLP library. It provides many industry-level methods to perform lemmatization. Unfortunately, spaCy has no module for stemming. To perform lemmatization, check out the below code:

```
#make sure to download the english model with "python -m spacy download en"
import en_core_web_sm
nlp = en_core_web_sm.load()
doc = nlp(u"""He determined to drop his litigation with the monastry, and relinguish his claims to the wood-cuting and fishery rihgts at once. He was the more ready to do this becuase the rights had become much less valuable, and he had indeed the vaguest idea where the wood and river in question were.""")
lemma_word1 = []
for token in doc: lemma_word1.append(token.lemma_) lemma_word1
```

Here *-PRON-* is the notation for pronoun which could easily be removed using regular expressions. **The benefit of spaCy is that we do not have to pass any pos parameter to perform lemmatization.**

-PRON- determine to drop -PRON- litigation with the monastry, and relinguish -PRON- claim to the wood-cuting and \n fishery rihgts at once. -PRON- be the more ready to do this becuase the right have become much less valuable, and -PRON- have \n indeed the vague idea where the wood and river in question b

3. Text Normalization using TextBlob

TextBlob is a Python library especially made for preprocessing text data. **It is based on the NLTK library**. We can use TextBlob to perform lemmatization. However, *there's no module for stemming in TextBlob.*

```
# from textblob lib import Word method from textblob import Word
text = """He determined to drop his litigation with the monastry, and relinguish his claims to the wood-cuting and fishery rihgts at once. He was the more ready to do this becuase the rights had become much less valuable, and he had indeed the vaguest idea where the wood and river in question were."""
lem = []
for i in text.split():
word1 = Word(i).lemmatize("n") word2 = Word(word1).lemmatize("v") word3 = Word(word2).lemmatize("a")
lem.append(Word(word3).lemmatize())
print(lem)
```

He determine to drop his litigation with the monastry, and relinguish his claim to the wood- cuting and fishery rihgts at once. He wa the more ready to do this becuase the right have become much le valuable, and he have indeed the vague idea where the wood and river in question were.

4.6 WORD CLOUD

Word Clouds came out to be a game-changer visualization technique for understanding and determining patterns and evolving trends. Whether to discover the political agendas of aspiring election candidates of a country or to analyze the customer reviews on the recently launched product, one can get a visual representation by plotting the Word Cloud.

Word Cloud or Tag Clouds is a visualization technique for texts that are natively used for visualizing the tags or keywords from the websites. These keywords typically are single words that depict the context of the webpage the word cloud is being made from. These words are clustered together to form a Word Cloud.

Each word in this cloud has a variable font size and color tone. Thus, this representation helps to determine words of prominence. A bigger font size of a word portrays its prominence more relative to other words in the cluster. Word Cloud can be built in varying shapes and sizes based on the creators' vision. The number of words plays an important role while creating a Word Cloud. More number of words does not always mean a better Word Cloud as it becomes cluttery and difficult to read. A Word Cloud must always be semantically meaningful and must represent what it is meant for.

Although, there are different ways by which Word Clouds can be created but the most widely used type is by using the **Frequency of Words** in our corpus. And thus, we will be creating our Word Cloud by using the Frequency type.

Applications

1. Customer's Feedback

Word Clouds are widely being used in industries by stakeholders to analyze the feedback received from end-users. Assume that a business launches a product and wants to know customer's feedback. Say the firm received 1000 feedbacks from different users. It would be very difficult for the stakeholders to read and make note of every feedback. Thus, Word Cloud would play a key role in getting top keywords among the feedback. This would help the firm determine if the feedback is positives or negatives and respective areas of improvement.

For example, A firm 'ABC' released a new Television, and based on the feedback received, the firm can make changes accordingly in the next series of Televisions.

2. Political Agenda of Candidates

Often the candidates of elections keep a checklist of agenda to talk about during the campaigns. Thus, the candidate's support team would analyze the candidate's speech and create a Word Cloud to select words for the next speech to keep a balance of agenda checklist. Analysts often create a Word Cloud of candidate's speeches from different parties to analyze and produce results to let people know which candidate is focusing on what areas of improvisation.

3. Trending Topics

Advertising Agencies would often need to know what is trending to create the next advertisement in context with trending topics. For example, Amul comes up with a creative advertisement based on the current issue or trend.

A Word Cloud in Python can be created in the following steps:

1. Import Necessary Libraries

Import the following libraries which are required to create a Word Cloud

```
import pandas as pd
import matplotlib.pyplot as plt from wordcloud import WordCloud
```

2. Selecting the Dataset

For this example, we are using Popular Dataset **Top Games on Google Play Store** from Kaggle.

Download the Dataset and save it in your current working directory for hassle-free code implementation. Import the dataset into a variable of your choice. Here our data is imported to variable **df**.

Text for the Word Cloud does not need to be from a Dataset. To get a meaningful text with fewer efforts, we are using the Dataset for our example.

```
df = pd.read_csv("android-games.csv")
```

3. Selecting the Text and Amount of Text for Word Cloud

Selecting text for creating a Word Cloud is an important task. One must check for various factors for the selection of Text such as:

- Do we have Problem Statement?
- Does the Selected Text have meaning in it?
- Can we conclude the created Word Cloud?
- Does our Text have an adequate amount of Text?

Word Cloud requires text in an adequate amount. A large number of words would hinder the visual appearance of Word Cloud and a lesser number of words would make no sense.

We can use the .head() method of DataFrame to check the Columns and the type of data present in them. In our example, we have taken the column **category** as Text.

Since the columns category has a prefix of **GAME** before each category game, our Word Cloud would end up creating **GAME** as the most frequent word and Word Cloud will have no meaning in int. Thus, we will perform filtering while adding the **category** column to the Text.

4. Check for NULL values

It is required to check for the null values in our dataset as while creating the Word Cloud, it would not accept text with **nan** values.

```
df.isna().sum()
```

If our dataset had any NaN values, we need to treat the missing values accordingly. Fortunately, this dataset has no NaN values, thus we can move to the next step. If there are very few NaN values, it is always advisable to remove such rows as it would not affect the Word Cloud to a larger extent.

5. Adding Text to a Variable

Based on the parameters from Step 3, add the Text Data to a variable of your choice. Here, we are adding the data into variable **text.**

```
text = " ".join(cat.split()[1] for cat in df.category)
```

Since we need to filter the **GAME** from the category, we have split each row value and took the 2nd item, i.e. the category name from the **category** column.

6. Creating the Word Cloud

Create an object of class WordCloud with the name of your choice and call the generate() method. Here we have created the object with the name **word_cloud.**

WordCloud() takes several arguments as per the need. Here we are adding two arguments:

1. **collocations = False**, which will ignore the collocation words from the Text
2. **background_color = 'White'**, which will make the words look clearer

The .generate() method takes one argument of the **text** we created. In our case, we will give the **text** variable as an argument to .generate().

```
word_cloud = WordCloud(collocations = False, background_color = 'white').
generate(text)
```

7. Plotting the Word Cloud

Using the **.imshow()** method of matplotlib.pyplot to display the Word Cloud as an image. .imshow() takes several arguments, but in our example, we are taking two arguments:

1. **word_cloud** created in Step 5
2. interpolation = **'bilinear'**

Since we are creating an image with .imshow(), the resampling of the image is done as the image pixel size and screen resolution doesn't not match. This resampling is controlled with the **interpolation** argument to produce softer or crisper images as per our need. There are several types of interpolation available such as gaussian, quadric, bicubic. Here we are using **bilinear** interpolation.

Plotting the image with axis off as we don't want axis ticks in our image.

```
plt.imshow(wordcloud, interpolation='bilinear')
plt.axis("off")
plt.show()
import pandas as pd
import matplotlib.pyplot as plt
%matplotlib inline
from wordcloud import WordCloud
#Importing Dataset
df = pd.read_csv("android-games.csv")
 #Checking the Data
df.head()
 #Checking for NaN
values df.isna().sum()
```

```
#Removing NaN
Values
#df.dropna(inplace = True)
#Creating the text variable
text = " ".join(cat.split()[1] for cat in df.category)
# Creating word_cloud with text as argument in .generate() method
word_cloud = WordCloud(collocations = False, background_color
 = 'white').generate(text) # Display the generated Word Cloud
 plt.imshow(wordcloud,
interpolation='bilinear') plt.axis("off")
plt.show()
```

8. The Complete Code

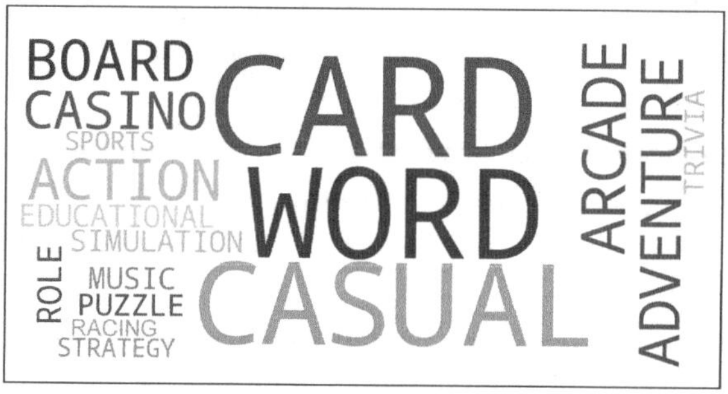

Figure 4.4

Word Cloud of **category** column (Image Source – Personal Computer) *The attached image size is irrespective of output image size Similarly, let's create Word Cloud for the **title** column from the imported dataset.

```
#Importing Libraries import pandas as pd
import matplotlib.pyplot as plt
%matplotlib inline
from wordcloud import WordCloud #Importing Dataset
df = pd.read_csv("1.csv") #Checking the Data df.head()
```

Figure 4.5

Word Cloud of title column (Image Source – Personal Computer) *The attached image size is irrespective of the output image size. Word Clouds created above can be customized further by adding advanced functionalities such as masking, contouring, and adjusting the cloud size. Word Clouds can be created not just using Python but other tools as well such as Microsoft Word, Business Intelligence Tools such as Tableau. There are currently numerous tools available on the internet that creates a Word Cloud just by giving the input text. Since the trend for the Word Cloud is increasing, the number of ways and tools are also increasing.

Word Cloud can be misleading sometimes. In few scenarios, it may happen that many words in our Word Cloud will have the same size, thus, it might get difficult to say which of them is more frequent than the other. We can use more advanced techniques to counter the problem.

4.7 TF-IDF

TF-IDF (Term Frequency-Inverse Document Frequency) is a way of measuring how relevant a word is to a document in a collection of documents.

This is done by multiplying two metrics:

- **Term Frequency (TF)**: how many times a word appears in a document.
- **Inverse Document Frequency (IDF)**: the inverse document frequency of the word across a collection of documents. Rare words have high scores, common words have low scores.

TF-IDF has many uses, such as in information retrieval, text analysis, keyword extraction, and as a way of obtaining numeric features from text for machine learning algorithms.

TF-IDF Origin

TF-IDF was first designed for document search and information retrieval, where a query is run and the system has to find the most relevant documents.

Suppose the query is the text "The bug". The system would give each document a higher score proportionally to the frequencies of the query words found in the document, weighting more rare words like "bug" with respect to common words like "the".

How to Compute TF-IDF?

Suppose we are looking for documents using the query *Q* and our database is composed of the documents *D1*, *D2*, and *D3*.

- ***Q*:** The cat.
- ***D1*:** The cat is on the mat.
- ***D2*:** My dog and cat are the best.
- ***D3*:** The locals are playing.

There are several ways of calculating TF, with the simplest being a raw count of instances a word appears in a document. We'll compute the TF scores using the ratio of the count of instances over the length of the document.

TF(word, document) = "number of occurrences of the word in the document" / "number of words in the document" Let's compute the TF scores of the words "the" and "cat" (i.e. the query words) with respect to the documents *D1*, *D2*, and *D3*.

TF("the", D1) = 2/6 = 0.33 TF("the", D2) = 1/7 = 0.14 TF("the", D3) = 1/4 = 0.25 TF("cat", D1) = 1/6 = 0.17 TF("cat", D2) = 1/7 = 0.14 TF("cat", D3) = 0/4 = 0

IDF can be calculated by taking the total number of documents, dividing it by the number of documents that contain a word, and calculating the logarithm. If the word is very common and appears in many documents, this number will approach 0. Otherwise, it will approach 1

IDF(word) = log(number of documents / number of documents that contain the word)

Let's compute the IDF scores of the words "the" and "cat". IDF("the") = log(3/3) = log(1) = 0

IDF("cat") = log(3/2) = 0.18

Multiplying TF and IDF gives the TF-IDF score of a word in a document. The higher the score, the more relevant that word is in that particular document.

TF-IDF(word, document) = TF(word, document) * IDF(word)

Let's compute the TF-IDF scores of the words "the" and "cat". TF-IDF("the", D1) = 0.33 * 0 = 0

TF-IDF("the, D2) = 0.14 * 0 = 0

TF-IDF("the", D3) = 0.25 * 0 = 0

TF-IDF("cat", D1) = 0.17 * 0.18= 0.0306

TF-IDF("cat, D2) = 0.14 * 0.18= 0.0252

TF-IDF("cat", D3) = 0 * 0 = 0

The next step is to use a ranking function to order the documents according to the TF-IDF scores of their words. We can use the average TF-IDF word scores over each document to get the ranking of *D1*, *D2*, and *D3* with respect to the query *Q*.

Average TF-IDF of D1 = (0 + 0.0306) / 2 = 0.0153

Average TF-IDF of D2 = (0 + 0.0252) / 2 = 0.0126

Average TF-IDF of D3 = (0 + 0) / 2 = 0

Looks like the word "the" does not contribute to the TF-IDF scores of each document. This is because "the" appears in all of the documents and thus it is considered a not-relevant word.

There are better-performing ranking functions in the literature, such as Okapi BM25. As a conclusion, when performing the query "The cat" over the collection of documents *D1*, *D2*, and *D3*, the ranked results would be:

1. *D1*: The cat is on the mat.
2. *D2*: My dog and cat are the best.
3. *D3*: The locals are playing.

The Use of TF-IDF in Machine Learning

TF-IDF is often used to transform text into a vector of numbers, otherwise known as text vectorization, where the numbers of the vectors are meant to somehow represent the content of the text. TF-IDF gives us a way to associate each word in a document with a number that represents how relevant each word is in that document. Such numbers can be then used as features of machine learning models.

4.8 SENTIMENT ANALYSIS – CASE STUDY

Sentiment analysis attaches a metric to a snippet of data that conveys how positive or negative its connotation is. It's deeper than the traditional customer survey that asks a participant to assign a value to a statement. The idea that "all press is good press" isn't quite accurate for any business looking to stay successful. If your customer sentiment around your brand is universally poor, your business may be in trouble.

You can apply sentiment analysis to unstructured data, such as the text of an email, a Facebook comment or a tweet. Through machine learning algorithms, sentiment analysis becomes more exact as the models consumer and analyzes and collects customer data.

Five Sentiment Analysis Use Cases

Businesses of every type can use sentiment analysis to gain deep insight into how their customers think and feel. But it's important to understand examples of how to use this strategy in order to execute it successfully. Here are some examples of sentiment analysis use cases that your business can use.

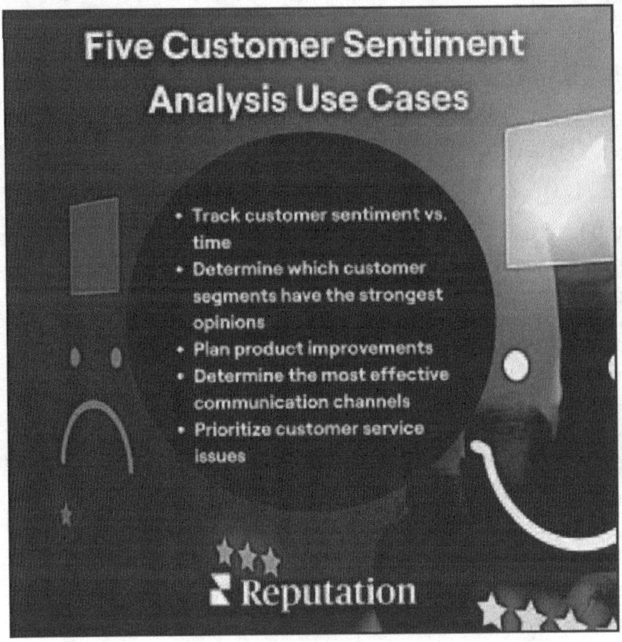

Figure 4.6

1. **Track Customer Sentiment vs. Time:** If your current data gathering indicates people are happy with your products and services, that's terrific. However, it can lead to complacency — sentiment analysis can prevent complacency by showing how customer sentiment tracks over time. For example, you could see an uptick in consumer sentiment and trace that data back to its most likely cause.
2. **Determine Which Customer Segments Have the Strongest Opinions:** Sentiment analysis can tell you which customers feel negatively about your brand for whatever reason. For example, you could find out that negative sentiment is coming from people who don't like your returns process. Likewise, sentiment analysis can help you identify which customers are your strongest brand ambassadors.

3. **Plan Product Improvements:** How have customers reacted to your product's new control layout? What specific product improvements put a smile on customers' faces?

   Sentiment analysis can use unstructured data to help you learn how people felt about your latest product release. This data could tell you that people love the product's appearance, but find that it is difficult to use. Sentiment analysis can tell you over time what complaints about "ease of use" are related to.
4. **Determine the Most Effective Communication Channels:** While consistency is important across communication channels, you may find that people respond more positively on some channels than others. Maybe the percentage of positive tweets about your brand is higher than the percentage of positive Facebook comments. Consider why that result might be. Such information can help you analyze how you interact with customers on various platforms, and make changes as necessary.
5. **Prioritize Customer Service Issues:** Customer support tickets tend to be answered in order of submission, but is that the best approach? Companies can use sentiment analysis to put top-priority customer service tickets at the head of the queue. Done strategically, this can help companies quickly address negative feedback.

Related: Customer Perception

What it is & How to improve it How Reputation can help you conduct Sentiment Analysis?

Getting started with conducting sentiment analysis requires that you analyze everywhere customers and potential leads are discussing your brand online. As we previously discussed, this includes:

- Social media
- All major online review sites
- Search results
- Business listings
- Custom survey data

This may produce an overwhelming amount of data. But Reputation offers sentiment analysis tools based in text analytics and deep learning. They will allow you to easily organize data in the best way to reveal your customer sentiment:

- **Word Cloud:** Reputation offers advanced analytics that produce a visual representation of your company's strengths and weaknesses. This can be viewed at a high level or for each location. See which words occur the most will give you an accurate read on how customers feel about your brand.
- **Tornado Chart:** Reputation's tornado chart is an alternate way to view those same analytics based on customer feedback across the web. This chart lists keywords vertically, with the most prominent term being listed in the longest bar at the top.

  The bars shrink as they go down, which makes them resemble a tornado. This is also benchmarked against the industry for comparison. That gives you a better understanding of customer sentiment overall and for individual locations.

- **Reputation Score:** The Reputation Score gives you a single number that lets you know how your brand is performing online. This is a real-time calculation based on a variety of factors that enables you to view and track sentiment. You can drill into this metric to see where your business is excelling and where there is room for improvement.
- **Flexible and Scalable Analytics:** Reputation offers a unique set of analytics that you won't find in other online reputation management solutions. You can customize your reports and views to obtain the most useful data that is specific to your business.

  Sentiment analysis is an essential tool for improving your online reputation. That's because it takes largely unstructured data and gives you actionable data that you can tactically and strategically address.

UNIT 5

Business Intelligence Strategy and Road Map

5.1 INTRODUCTION

What is Big Data?

Big data is a collection of large datasets that cannot be processed using traditional computing techniques. It is not a single technique or a tool, rather it has become a complete subject, which involves various tools, techniques and frameworks.

What Comes Under Big Data?

Big data involves the data produced by different devices and applications. Given below are some of the fields that come under the umbrella of Big Data.

- **Black Box Data:** It is a component of helicopters, airplanes, and jets, etc. It captures voices of the flight crew, recordings of microphones and earphones, and the performance information of the aircraft.
- **Social Media Data:** social media such as Facebook and Twitter hold information and views posted by millions of people across the globe.
- **Stock Exchange Data:** The stock exchange data holds information about the 'buy' and 'sell' decisions made on a share of different companies made by the customers.
- **Power Grid Data:** The power grid data holds information consumed by a particular node with respect to a base station.
- **Transport Data:**Transport data includes model, capacity, distance and availability of a vehicle.
- **Search Engine Data:** Search engines retrieve lots of data from different data bases.

Figure 5.1

Thus, Big Data includes huge volume, high velocity, and extensible variety of data. The data in it will be of three types.

- **Structured data:** Relational data.
- **Semi Structured data:** XML data.
- **Unstructured data:** Word, PDF, Text, Media Logs.

Benefits of Big Data

- Using the information kept in social networks like Facebook, marketing agencies learn about the responses for their campaigns, promotions, and other advertising mediums.
- Using the information in social media like preferences and product perception of their consumers, product companies and retail organizations are planning their production.
- Using the data regarding the previous medical history of patients, hospitals are providing better and quick service.

Big Data Technologies

Big data technologies are important in providing more accurate analysis, which may lead to more concrete decision-making resulting in greater operational efficiencies, cost reductions, and reduced risks for the business.

To harness the power of big data, you would require an infrastructure that can manage and process huge volumes of structured and unstructured data in real-time and can protect data privacy and security.

There are various technologies in the market from different vendors including Amazon, IBM, Microsoft, etc., to handle big data. While looking into the technologies that handle big data, we examine the following two classes of technology:

1. Operational Big Data

This include systems like MongoDB that provide operational capabilities for real-time, interactive workloads where data is primarily captured and stored.

NoSQL Big Data systems are designed to take advantage of new cloud computing architectures that have emerged over the past decade to allow massive computations to be run inexpensively and efficiently. This makes operational big data workloads much easier to manage, cheaper, and faster to implement.

Some NoSQL systems can provide insights into patterns and trends based on real-time data with minimal coding and without the need for data scientists and additional infrastructure.

2. Analytical Big Data

These includes systems like Massively Parallel Processing (MPP) database systems and MapReduce that provide analytical capabilities for retrospective and complex analysis that may touch most or all of the data.

MapReduce provides a new method of analyzing data that is complementary to the capabilities provided by SQL, and a system based on MapReduce that can be scaled up from single servers to thousands of high- and low-end machines.

These two classes of technology are complementary and frequently deployed together. Operational vs. Analytical Systems

Terms	Operational	Analytical
Latency	1 ms -100 ms	1 min -100 min
Concurrency	1000 -100,000	1 -10
AccessPattern	WritesandReads	Reads
Queries	Selective	Unselective
DataScope	Operational	Retrospective
EndUser	Customer	DataScientist
Technology	NoSQL	MapReduce,MPPDatabase

What are the Characteristics of Big Data?

Three characteristics define big data: volume, variety, and velocity.

Together, these characteristics define **"BigData".** They have created the need for anew class of capabilities to augment the way things are done today to provide a better line of sight and control over our existing knowledge domains and the ability to act on them.

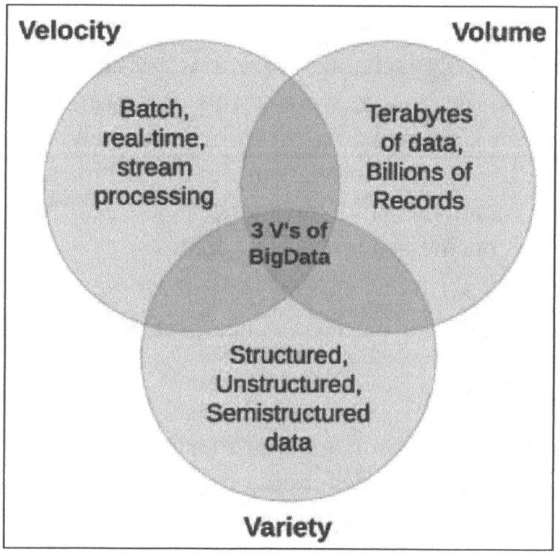

Figure 5.2

1. The Volume of Data

The sheer volume of data being stored today is exploding. In the year2000,800,000petabytes (PB) of data were stored in the world. Of course, a lot of the data that's being created today isn't analyzed at all and that's another problem that needs to be considered. This number is expected to reach 35 zettabytes (ZB) by 2020.

Twitter alone generates more than 7 terabytes (TB) of data every day, Facebook 10 TB, and some enterprises generate terabytes of data every hour of every day of the year. It's no longer unheard of for individual enterprises to have storage clusters holding petabytes of data.

Figure 5.3

Source

When you stop and think about it, it's a little wonder we're drowning in data. We store everything: environmental data, financial data, medical data, surveillance data, and the list goes on and on. For example, taking your smartphone out of your holster generates an event; when your commuter train's door opens for boarding, that's an event; check-in for a plane, badge into work, buy a song on iTunes, change the TV channel, take an electronic toll route— every one of these actions generates data.

Okay, you get the point: There's more data than ever before and all you have to do is look at the terabyte penetration rate for personal home computers as the telltale sign. We used to keep a list of all the data warehouses we knew that surpassed a terabyte almost a decade ago—suffice to say, things have changed when it comes to volume.

As implied by the term "Big Data," organizations are facing massive volumes of data. Organizations that don't know how to manage this data are overwhelmed by it. But the opportunity exists, with the right technology platform, to analyze almost all of the data (or at least more of it by identifying the data that's useful to you) to gain a better understanding of your business, your customers, and the marketplace. And this leads to the current conundrum facing today's businesses across all industries.

As the amount of data available to the enterprise is on the rise, the percent of data it can process, understand, and analyze is on the decline, thereby creating the blind zone.

What's in that Blind Zone?

You don't know: it might be something great or maybe nothing at all, but the "don't know "is the problem (or the opportunity, depending on how you look at it). The conversation about data volumes has changed from terabytes to petabytes with an inevitable shift to zettabytes, and all this data can't be stored in your traditional systems.

2. The Variety of Data

Source

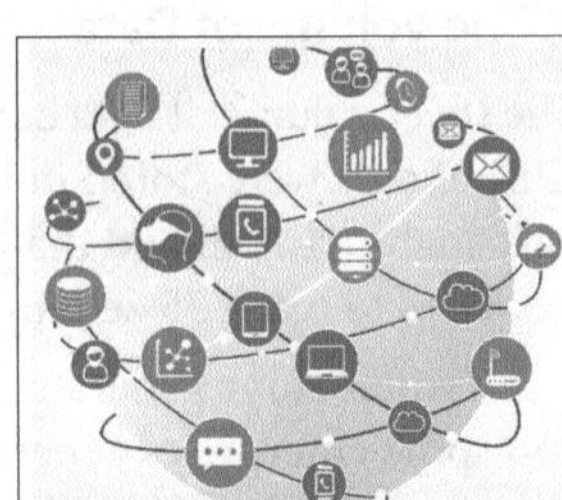

Figure 5.4

The volume associated with the Big Data phenomena brings along new challenges for data centers trying to deal with it: **its variety**.

With the explosion of sensors, and smart devices, as well as social collaboration technologies, data in an enterprise has become complex, because it includes not only traditional relational data, but also raw, semi-structured, exponential growth of business activities and transactions, log data can become a huge headache to be stored, processed, and presented in the most efficient, cost-effective manner.

Many commercial and open-source log analytics tools can provide you the ability to collect, process, and analyze massive log data without having to dump the data into relational databases and retrieve it through SQL queries. The synergy between log search capabilities and big data analytics has enabled organizations to discover insights for more agile operations. Big data log analytics applications are now widely used for various business goals, from IT system security and network performance to market trends and e-commerce personalization.

Usecase#2: E-Commercepersonalization

Remember when you were leisurely (or frantically)browsing online shopping sites to find that perfect gift for a friend or family member (or yourself)? How often do you type in the search box, click on the navigation bar, expand product descriptions, or add a product to your cart? If you were an e-commerce company, every one of these actions can become the key to optimizing the entire shopping experience. And thus, the daunting tasks of collecting, processing, and analyzing shoppers' behavior and transaction data open up enormous opportunities for big data in e-commerce.

A powerful search and big data analytics platform allows e-commerce companies to (1) clean and enrich product data for a better search experience on both desktops and mobile devices; and (2) use predictive analytics and machine learning to predict user preferences through log data, then personalize products in a most-likely-to-buy order that maximizes conversion. There has also been a new movement towards real-time e-commerce personalization enabled by big data's massive processing power.

Usecase#3: Recommendation Engines

If you've been on online media streaming platforms, you may have noticed those "recommended for you" videos, movies, or music. Doesn't it feel great to have a selection personalized only for you? It's easy. It's time-saving.

Overall, a satisfying user experience, right? Have you also noticed that the more videos and movies you watched, the better those recommendations became? As the media and entertainment space is filled by strong competitors, the ability to deliver the top user experience will be the winning factor.

Big data, with its scalability and power to process massive amounts of both structured (e.g. video titles users search for, music genre they prefer) and unstructured data (e.g. user viewing/listening patterns), can enable companies to analyze billions of clicks and viewing data from you and other users like you for the best recommendations. Over time, through machine learning and predictive analytics, the recommendations become better tailored to the user's taste.

Usecase#4: Automated can did Ate Placement In Recruiting

Recruiters often feel they don't have the(right)tools in the race to place candidates as quickly as possible in a competitive environment. As matching resume keywords with job descriptions no longer provide the desired results, new approaches to using big data for recruiting have allowed recruiters to speed up and automate the placement process like never before.

A big data recruitment platform can mine from internal databases and provide a 360-degree view of a candidate, such as education, experience, skill sets, job titles, certifications, geography, and anything else recruiters can think of, then compare them to the company's past hiring experience, salaries, previously successful candidates, etc. to identify the "best match." These platforms can even go beyond matching to anticipate recruiting needs and suggest candidates before positions are posted, allowing recruiters to be more proactive – a competitive edge against their competitors.

Usecase#5: Insurance Fraud Detection

Organizations that handle large numbers of financial transactions continue searching for more innovative, effective approaches to fight fraud. Medical insurance agencies are no exception, as fraud can cost the industry up to $5 billion annually. In the traditional fraud detection model, fraud investigators need to work with BI analysts or uncomplex SQL queries from bill and claim data, then wait weeks or months to get the results back. This process sometimes causes lengthy delays in legal fraud cases, thus, huge losses for businesses.

With big data technologies, billions of billings and claim records can be processed and pulled into a search engine, so that investigators can analyze individual records by performing intuitive searches on a graphical interface. Predictive analytics and machine learning capabilities enable a big data platform for fraud detection to provide automatic red flag alerts as soon as it recognizes a pattern that matches a previously known fraud scheme.

Usecase#6: Relevancy and Retention Boost for Online Publishing

For research publishing companies, giving their online subscribers the right content, they want is critical to building authority, expanding the subscriber base, and boosting the bottom line. In addition to investing in great SEO efforts to make the publishing site searchable, strategizing how well the content can be served once users are on the website is a primary factor impacting conversion and repeat business.

With the rise of personalization, big data brings a new paradigm for processing and analyzing both content data (authors, titles, topics) and user data (document downloads, preferences). First, a powerful search engine helps clean and enrich research documents' metadata to ensure users find the most relevant content and explore related content easily. Then, through machine learning and predictive analytics, the publisher will be able to serve content in a particular order in which the user's favorite content appears in the top results. How do they know for sure? Because they can repeatedly test and score the search engine's performance offline to predict search accuracy and abandonment rates before putting the engine into production on the live website.

As social, cloud, and information have become the driving forces of modern business, we expect to see more and more innovative use cases that leverage search and big data analytics to make sense and make use of the vast amount of data. Like the cloud, big data is here to stay and continue to enrich the business technology ecosystem in the coming years.